I believe everyone has at least one good book tucked inside of them. A story to tell. A journey to unfold. Words on a page that speak life to life. As our own worst critic, one might surmise their book to be insignificant, not quite a page turner or perhaps a story already told countless times before. Then there's that moment. The moment that defines our uniqueness as individuals, and therefore the awe-inspiring beauty of our own story! For me, August 15, 2013, gave birth to that moment. Years later, a very pregnant version of myself sits at the computer to tell of this moment. As my daughter grows inside of me, I am emboldened to share such a painful event as to hopefully educate the universe and protect someone else's daughter (or son) from the horror of gaslighting.

Here's the moment that forever changed the trajectory of my life and redefined the passion I have for life.

WHITE
SOCKS

THE PASSION OF THE PROCESS

RECOGNIZING, RECKONING WITH, AND
RE-DISCOVERING LIFE AFTER GASLIGHTING

KL HIGDON, PHARM.D., BCPS

This is a work of nonfiction. Howbeit, some of the names and identifying characteristics of individuals involved, and geographical locations have been changed in order to disguise their identities. Any resulting resemblance to persons living or dead in entirely coincidental and unintentional.

The subject matter provided in this book is not intended as a substitute for consultation or treatment with a qualified mental health professional. Neither the publisher nor author takes any responsibility for any possible consequences from any treatment, action, or applications thereof apropos any person reading or following the information in this book.

This book contains subject matter related to mental health, suicide, and sexual trauma. Reader discretion advised.

Cover Design by Candace Martin.

Author's Photo:
Anna Hall Photography
Make up by Victoria Phillips
Coiffurist Tomeika Myers

Hudson Publishing, LLC

ISBN:
Paperback: 979-8-9869371-0-6
Hardback: 979-8-9869371-2-0
eBook: 979-8-9869371-3-7

www.runchilerun.com
Facebook.com/KLHigdon
@KLHigdon

It was good...

Contents

THE GOSPEL
Now I want you to know, brothers and sisters, that what has happened to me has actually served to advance the gospel.

Philippians 1:12 New International Version

Popcorn Paint

T he brightness of the ceiling light had awakened me to a nightmare. I lay there dazed by the night, the glare of the light, and the popcorn paint of my grandmother's ceiling. My mother was sitting at the edge of the bed, hemorrhaging, blood pouring from her wrists and upper thighs. I could see the dark of night through the bedroom window and the light of the street lamp. And my mother, just sitting there, disconnected and totally unfazed by the blood. There she sat, counting her fingers aloud, using the index finger of one hand to singularly touch the fingers of the other hand. My eyes raced around the room, searching for understanding of what had transpired. My eyes fixed on the bloody blade resting next to her. I could not understand what was happening but I was afraid—afraid of the unknown, afraid for me and my brother, afraid for my mother.

I gently woke my younger brother who was sleeping alongside me and my mother in the king size bed. My brother and I exited the bed to the left, carefully walked around the foot of the bed, and quietly passed our mother who was still sitting there with this bizarre look on her face, all the while bleeding and counting. I hurried us up the burgundy-carpeted hallway to my grandmother's bedroom. Her room was no more than 20 feet away, but the distance seemed interminable. I shook my grandmother awake and beckoned for her to help. I still hear my grandmother's voice as she entered the bedroom from which my brother and I had just fled…the consternation in her tone as she called out my mother's name and asked her what she had done.

This was not an isolated event, as my childhood years were marked by a mother who had made several attempts to end her own life. Her nightstand was routinely decorated with antidepressant, anxiolytic, and antipsychotic medications. She would return home from one inpatient treatment just to be readmitted for another overdose or suicide attempt. She was seemingly in constant emotional turmoil, detached from reality. This time, this night, however, was exceptionally different. There was the one time our weeknight church service had been interrupted with notice of my mother being rushed to the hospital to "have her stomach pumped." She'd overdosed on pills, a dreadful event in and of itself, but still not quite as remarkable as *this* night. When she'd overdosed on the pills, I had not physically been there to see her illness at work … had not experienced the horror first hand … had no visual images to long to erase. This time, this night, however, was definitely different and a time I'd never forget.

Dolan Hudson

L ong before the birth of our modern day supers and their super villains lived my grandmother, this super bad ass powerhouse of a woman standing tall against the challenges of everyday real life and looking flawless all the while doing so. Dolan Hudson was the kind of woman that superheroes are crafted from and lyrical beats are set to. She was the epitome of strength and her day-to-day life spoke to ballads like Chaka Khan's *I'm Every Woman*. Indeed, Dolan walked to the beat of her own drum. She was resilient, indestructible, and a way maker. As far back as I can remember, she'd always had this robust figure and these big hands that told a story of their own, a story of tireless hours spent working in the fields in the deep south of Georgia, picking cotton. Born in 1925, this woman had known hard work and had surely faced her own share of hard times. Nevertheless, I never heard her complain, never saw my grandmother cry, never saw her bend at the mercy of difficulty, never saw her buckle under pressure. We're all born fearless, but I'm convinced Dolan had sprung forth from her mother's womb cloaked in a brilliant red cape that galloped in the wind behind her. She was unwavering, simply extraordinary.

My grandmother loved God in this absolutely crazy way. Her faith was her anchor, the very foundation by which she cultivated life and love. As a child, I'd sit with her on her front porch, eating from the pits of these huge, richly sweet watermelons and listen to her talk of God. She'd talk about Him like He was this person she'd hang out with, shucking collards and shelling peas. She didn't quote scripture, chapter, or verse. She spoke, instead, of God like she'd met Him before and had sat face-to-face with Him, sipping coffee and reminiscing of times past. She spoke of Him in this deeply personal way, like He was this chill friend that she could call up and crack jokes with or that neighbor she could borrow a cup of sugar from. My grandmother had this intimate relationship with God that spoke to her super powers and ability to brave the world. According to my grandmother, He was this "lily of the valley" and her "bridge over troubled waters."

I remember having this little suitcase that read *Going to Grandma's*. Even at such a young age, I'd often think this suitcase should simply read *Grandma's* as that's where my brother and I spent the bulk of our earliest years. My father was busily chasing the next youngest skirt tail, so my maternal grandmother took care of my brother and me. My grandparents had strategically bought my mother a home only one street over from theirs, so the frequent transitions between my mother's home and grandparents' were physically easy but not any less emotionally taxing. There was no change in school zone, no disruption in the bus I'd get on, no friendships to forcibly end and new ones to begin. There was just the corrosive effect of my mother's mental illness that could not be displaced by geography.

With eight children and thirteen grandchildren in and out of the house, Dollie—what I grew to call my grandmother—cooked all the time. (I didn't know what it meant to "eat out" until college.) And as the youngest granddaughter, my post was in the kitchen. On Friday nights, I helped clean the freshly caught catfish, and on any other given day, I was peeling and dicing potatoes, washing greens, shelling early peas, or deep frying chicken. There was no such thing as a dishwasher. That beautiful gadget was the set of hands God had given me, this commercial size Joy' brand dish detergent, and a dishcloth. If I wasn't helping to cook, my step stool and I were elbow deep washing dishes. We Hudsons were a big family, and with the majority of her children living only minutes away from her doorstep, my grandmother's home was our core— the gathering place, the heart of the Hudson family. And her kitchen was its soul.

Dolan had the natural tendency to cook these extra large meals—two different kinds of meats, on average four vegetables, and at minimum two breads (with one of those breads certain to be cornbread). She cooked in these industrial style, restaurant sized pots and pans. There was always more than enough. Dollie lived out a simple philosophy. We *are* our brother's keeper. All of Tenth Street and the surrounding neighborhoods respected Mrs. Hudson, as she fed everyone and genuinely cared about every single person. I loved helping her cook (even had a couple of aprons to complement hers), enjoyed helping her "fix plates," and actually understood, even then, the impact my grandmother had on other people's lives as I'd run those hot plates up and down Tenth Street. Every day with Dolan was subject to the principles of a soup kitchen or Meals on Wheels. What she had, she shared, and what she didn't have, she'd create. Before I knew what the word *philanthropy* meant or what it meant to be a humanitarian, there was my grandmother. Though never presented with any accolades or interviewed to tell her story, this amazing woman lived a life that speaks to the values, discipline, and calling of our modern day hero. Dolan was a trailblazer and, as interesting as it might sound, changed lives right there through the gift of her kitchen. She fed people that otherwise would have gone hungry, a humbling act of kindness and evidence of God's grace. As one of the most revered elders of our neighborhood, Dolan instilled in me this principle that I call *the Hudson Way*: "You must have enough food on hand to *whip up* a meal in case the pastor drops by." Translation: It's cool to have enough for you and yours, but it's life-changing to provide for someone else.

By age eleven, I could *whip up* a complete Dolan-style meal, a faculty that would serve me well in my adult life and in my relationships. More importantly, I had begun to pattern my personality and character after that of my grandmother. Life with my parents and life following their divorce was turbulent, constant theatrics at best. My grandmother, however, was this symbol of peace. One of the things I cherished most about her was her genuine care for others. Dolan cared for total strangers, something that I believe had to do with her own beginnings. My grandmother was from the small community of Matthews, Georgia, home of a little more than one hundred people. I can only imagine that in such a close-knit population nearly everyone is regarded as family and treated as such. Dolan would welcome a total stranger into her home, allow him or her to sit at her table, and she would feed them. I mean, there is just something personal about someone eating at your table...not to mention, that someone being someone you don't know.

This amazing woman believed we were "all God's chillen," and it was God's will that we treat one another as such. I'd watch as Dolan handed out the last dollar she'd secretly stashed away in her bra. She wasn't the least worried about where that money would in turn come from or how the next bill would be paid. Dolan knew God to be Jehovah Jireh, a constant provider. She'd brought my cousins, my brother, and me up in a traditional Southern Baptist church where the deacons raised hymns in worship and actually got down on their knees to pray. And on any given day, the pastor, himself, could be found visiting with the sick and shut in. Dolan was grounded, rooted in her faith, and, accordingly, so were we. (This was simply not a negotiable thing in the Hudson house. You loved God. Period. No discussion.) My grandmother was a good person. I loved this woman and everything she stood for. Hard working, strong-willed, strong-minded, smart, caring, and loving. And her smile ... she had this smile that was as delightful as the peppermint candy she'd quietly slip me during church service. Amid the unpredictables afforded to us by this thing called life, I am confident I could not have chosen a more spirited person from whom to pattern my life. In my grandmother, I saw God's truest, purest, most human form. I grabbed hold of this and used it to shape the cornerstones of my being.

In the eyes of Dolan Hudson, three things of absolute no compromise were God, discipline, and education. Phenomenal she was, and likewise, an enforcer. Dolan had seen her own fair share of struggles and had worked hard to pave the way for our generation to not ever meet her adversities. I remember the stories my grandmother used to tell me as I was seated on her burgundy carpet, legs crossed one over the other, her greasing my scalp. I'd always had this long, thick, coarse hair (aka nappy hair), and my scalp was oftentimes layered with what my grandmother called "growing dandruff." This time together was a ritualistic process and time well spent as Dolan would use a small-tooth comb to scratch up my dandruff, lifting the itchy nuisance from the base of my scalp and gliding it along the shaft of my hair until the worn towel draping my shoulders was sprinkled with silver flakes. She'd then apply a fresh layer of grease to my scalp. As I sat at her feet, Dolan would live out loud with me the memories of her having to pick cotton, sometimes with her children working alongside her. By the age of 18, my grandmother had married and given birth to her first child, so work was this very real presence in her life. Beyond the fields, she'd worked for decades as an orderly at Gracewood State School and Hospital. Her experiences, her life, her work spoke to Horace Mann's position on education as "the great equalizer".[1] Day in and day out, my grandmother had reminded me that I was to "go to school" and "get a good education."

On the heels of graduation, I was amped about life and my career. During my undergraduate years at Paine College, I'd founded a recycling initiative called the E.A.R.T.H. Club (Environmental Advocates Recycling To Help save our College) and maintained an active role in mentoring youth. I'd been privileged to pledge one of the most esteemed sororities and represent the student body as its queen. My grandmother was most proud as I floated across the stage as class salutatorian. Case in point, I was pumped! All of the studying, all of the sacrifices, all of the summer programs I'd attended during high school summer breaks, and all the college credits earned from these programs had spoken for *this* moment. I was proud of myself, proud of my hard work, proud of my accomplishments. Next on my life-to-do-list was medical school and a career in obstetrics and gynecology. I thought I'd had this thing called life all figured out until God showed up and called an audible .

ॐ

White Coats

My mother was as equally obsessed with education as was my grandmother, a gift that had helped me stay focused and centered on academics. This focus aligned me with a professor whose commitment to research and pharmacy practice forever changed the optics of my world. The summer before graduating from Paine, I'd worked as a research apprentice at the local medical college, an opportunity that introduced me to Dr. Kash Auvi. This woman was smart, innovative, and captivating, known around the globe for her research in stroke therapy and outcomes. It was certainly an understatement to say that I was intrigued by her work. Up to this point, I didn't have any interest in pharmacy and definitely no interest in learning about stroke. Yet, here I was, magnetically drawn to this clinician's intellect and enthralled with everything I'd come to learn. Prior to meeting Dr. Auvi, I'd never stepped foot into a research laboratory, never analyzed an investigational study, never been published. These attainments sparked the start of something amazing!

Under Dr. Auvi's tutelage, I published my first manuscript, ditched my plans for medical school, and applied to pharmacy school. Dr. Auvi had breathed fresh air into this stale concept called pharmacy. Pharmacy, for me, had been this box-style, generic construct where this stoic person could always be found staring at a computer, willfully not making eye contact. With

Dr. Auvi, I'd discovered pharmacy to be this life-like body, the pulse of medicine and rich with purpose. Pharmacy was so much more than pills in a bottle or the druggist standing behind the counter. It was, indeed, the very heart of medicine. Hit television shows had done a great job depicting medical doctors on hospital rounds, standing at the patient's bedside, draped in long white coats and stethoscopes. And then there were the doctors racing down the hallways, answering the call to save a life. But there wasn't much face time given to the other characters rockin' the white coats. With Dr. Auvi, those white coats assumed true identities and came alive as pharmacists—pharmacists that stood front and center with the team, on rounds, offering up alternative therapies for the patient. And then there was the pharmacist racing to answer the call *with* the code team, armed with lifesaving pharmacologic artillery. Pharmacy was so much more than what I'd experienced in the local venues. There were oh so many facets—hospital pharmacy, retail pharmacy, community pharmacy, nuclear pharmacy, and so much more! I loved this dynamic and was more than thankful for the life-changing exposure. My twenty-year old life had more than leveled up. It had been catapulted to a whole new dimension.

White Coat Ceremony 2002 found me seated in an auditorium at the University of Georgia College of Pharmacy. I was surrounded by a group of my peers, a diverse class of a little more than 100 individuals representing all parts of the globe and all eager to take on the rigorous challenges of our doctoral program. I'd survived the grueling application process, managed to not embarrassingly pass out in my interview, and was now basking in the bliss of my acceptance into the university. I was now ready to take on the newness of two-hour lectures, the steep learning curve of pharmacology, and the infamous beast known as pharmacokinetics. When

I wasn't in class, the lab, or tutoring, I could be found in the local bookstore, studying to the sultry sounds of Norah Jones and Jack Johnson while at other times, silently transcribing my recorded lectures. At least one day a week, time could place me in my little red car, jamming to the melodies of Sara Bareilles and making the 100-mile commute to work. Time management was no stranger to me as I'd learned early on how to juggle school in the ever-present moment of life and particularly how to do so effectively. Aside from school and work, there were the extracurricular activities like the pharmacy fraternity and the professional organizations that kept me very busy yet more marketable in the growing, competitive field. I had no time for any serious relationship to obfuscate my view. I was deeply committed to my education and deeply entangled in this love affair with work. I was in focus, and my life was, for once, in balance.

Fourth year of pharmacy school landed me back in my hometown, completing clinical rotations. I'd lived on campus during my undergraduate years and continued to board away from my mother's residence even upon this return. I'd seemingly escaped my childhood vicissitudes and was happy with the course God had set my life upon. Having spent three years away from the only place I'd called home had taught me a lot! I'd learned much, both in and out of the classroom. Perhaps the most valuable lessons I'd garnered, however, were those in the study of self and my own proclivities. I'd transitioned from an undergraduate classroom size averaging twenty students to operating at the university level with more than 100 different people and personalities. I'd never had much of a competitive spirit, but I'd quickly learned how to be assertive, fiercely independent, and grounded. I'd developed my own sense of style and established my own identity, with notable flakes of Dolan speckled throughout. I valued being kind to others, enjoyed chatting with strangers, and found joy in doing the unexpected (like paying for the groceries of the veteran in line behind me or picking up the tab of a random family in a restaurant). In all my growth and learning, I'd never lost sight of my grandmother's teachings, and I could hear her spirit resonate in mine, "You never know what a person is going through." So for no reason other than waking up each morning, I'd chosen joy and happiness as the hallmark of my personality.

&

Blue Scrubs

C linicals had pulled us out of the monotony of the classroom and placed us center field amid the action. This was prime time to test our skills, build mental fortitude, and exercise those recall muscles. For the next several weeks, I'd rotate through a number of disciplines and be *tested* in a sundry of capacities ... the greatest of these *tests* made manifest in a human form and unlike anything I'd ever known. I'd kept running into this guy in the hospital. He was dressed in blue scrubs and seemed to coincidentally be in the same spaces as I. I'd see him on my way to morning rounds, in the cafeteria, or leaving my preceptor's office. We'd not exchanged more than a head nod and continued in this fashion until working together on a code. On this particular day, Code Blue had been activated for a patient in cardiopulmonary arrest. As an intern on critical care, it was my responsibility to answer the call with the code team. After the patient had been stabilized, the team was debriefed. Again, I was Miss Assertive, and in being such, I'd seized this opportunity to finally approach this guy and engage in friendly conversation. He'd smiled, introduced himself, and said, "We have to stop meeting this way." I wasn't one for placating gender roles so I followed through with, "Yeah, maybe we should go to dinner sometime."

He was in his third year of medicine, busy preparing for step 2 of the medical licensing exam and mapping out plans for residency. He'd appeared so charming, compassionate, and kind … maple sweet. He was the perfect gentleman, opening doors ahead of my entry, displaying chivalry at every turn. He'd fold his arms across his body as we talked, gently nodding his head to the conversation. His smile flashed all his teeth and unveiled the dimples hidden in his cheeks. He had this essential tremor that added a layer of softness to his demeanor. His clothes were always perfectly pressed, even his jeans with the most perfect creases. His shoes always shiny. His fedora perfectly aligned. He was well versed and always well spoken … polished. Everything about him spoke of perfection with this alluring effect.

Like me, this guy in the blue scrubs was from humble beginnings. He was from the small town of Lodebar and had attributed his passion for medicine to his mother, who had single-handedly raised him, his older sister, and his younger brother. He'd shared with me that he had also grown up with a dad that had chosen philandering over the commitments of marriage and how his father's indiscretions had resulted in extramarital children and an onslaught of pain and emotional mayhem. He'd shared with me how this emotional distress had been made manifest in the academic performance and behavior of his younger brother who later had to be homeschooled. And like my mother, his mother too, however secretly, battled the wages of emotional warfare. His *story* was so touching; it tugged at the strings of my heart. He was his family's golden child—accomplished, well liked, well known, and destined to be the most successful. In the midst of our getting to know one another, this guy in the blue scrubs had once told me that if he'd not chosen medicine, he'd have pursued acting … he and his brother even had these elaborate fictitious characters (an ornery old man named Willie and a lavish young pimp known as Tasco) that they had created and would often play out. I was surprised at the sound of such an antithetical career choice, but unknowingly would later come to appreciate the flair for showmanship that hid this guy's true identity.

What had begun as a free dinner date, compliments of the drug rep industry, grew into a financially exhaustive relationship. The first few months of our courtship seemed "normal," with the ritualistic date nights and seamless late night phone conversations. We were both students, yet I was the only one working and unrecognizably fronting most of our expenses. I was rounding the bend of fourth year and eagerly looking forward to graduation and the post graduate, year-one residency program that would ensue. Months preceding my graduation, the guy in the blue scrubs, came to me with this convincing story about his troublesome finances. He'd run out of money to pay for housing and medical school. He'd offered up a reasonable explanation for why each member of his immediate family circle was unable to help him, spanning from his mother's own financial strain to his sister's already overly compromised budget. The guy in the blue scrubs and I were now in a relationship... a team. And if anyone understood the struggle, it was I. After all, I was a working student with an insurmountable debt in federal and private student loans. So I resolved to do the only thing I knew how to do. I was the product of Dolan Hudson, raised up to care, raised up to be compassionate, raised up to be my brother's keeper. I was galvanized to act! I would help this guy in the blue scrubs. Here was the plan. He'd move in to my place, and I'd have my grandmother do for him what she'd done for me, co-sign for private student loans. His problems...solved.

May 2006, I'd graduated magna cum laude from the University of Georgia with my doctorate degree in pharmacy. I'd worked hard for this epic moment and celebrated the culmination of my career with my grandmother, family, friends, and the guy in the blue scrubs. Only months prior to this big day, I'd met my guy's mother and was enamored when she'd told me I was the first girl he'd ever brought home. My guy was 28 years old, so me being the girl that he'd chosen to finally bring home to mama was a big deal… or so I thought. The mendacity of his mother's nature would lie in wait as I continued on this path of loving her son. For now, me and my guy would continue to live together while I worked as a post-graduate intern, studied for and took my pharmacy board examinations, and awaited the start of residency. At the same time, my guy would prep for post-graduate training and the residency interviews that lie ahead.

Yes

Match Day. The long-awaited moment for medical students. This is the day when shit gets real… when medical students learn their fate and where it is they will spend the next four years in residency training. This is a much-celebrated moment across the states, as tens of thousands of students, foreign and domestic, vie for these spots. I'd accompanied my guy to countless interviews with bated anticipation that I'd join him as a fellow second year postgraduate resident and as his partner for life. We'd been having *the* talk… the what-happens-next talk, a conversation that brought with it so much appeal, so much excitement. The exhilaration, however, was often times snuffed out when my guy showed no interest in making home anywhere close to Augusta. From Anderson, South Carolina to Alabama, he was the least interested in a place that we could make our own. My guy was homebound with the Southwest Georgia Family Medicine Program set in his crosshairs. This program offered no pharmacy practice residency, no opportunity for me to grow, as there was not even a neighboring program for me to seek out. Life in Lodebar for me would be that of a working woman, one whose dreams of continued educational growth would have to take a backseat to her guy's ambitions. I knew all this, the immense weight such evidences put forth. I hated tussling with my gut, yet when my guy had proposed the eve of Match Day, I'd said, "Yes!"

He was one for the romantic flare. He'd "asked" my parents for permission and set the stage for the big moment at his and his family's favorite beach getaway, St. Simon's Island. As we made the more than three-hour drive from Augusta to the island, I'd begun to play out the events in the evening's forecast. I wasn't one for surprises and couldn't help but think that with the timing—Thursday evening, only hours before Match Day—this was it! And indeed, it was. Scripted. There was the grand hotel... the walk on the beach... the down-on-one-knee lighthouse proposal. The only thing missing was the dramatic music one would find in theatre. And just like that, I'd surrendered. I'd said yes to leaving my family and friends behind and making the assured move to more than 200 miles away. I'd said yes to being content with having completed only one year postgraduate residency training. I'd said yes to not pursuing my own dreams, yes to tabling my personal goals. I'd said yes to living our life his way and yes to being okay with that.

The months that followed our engagement were slated for great things. My fiancé would walk in May. My post-doctoral residency program would conclude in June. And then, there was the wedding. Living with a man you weren't married to was darn near criminal in the eyes of Dolan Hudson. This woman was "ol school" and definitely not a fan of "shackin' up," something that, for some time now, I'd concealed from her. I was sure, however, not to be so fortuitous when moving so far away. The date was set. We'd move in June, wed in December.

Summer 2007, we'd planted our roots in Lodebar, and closed on our first home, compliments of the generous sign-on bonus I'd been awarded as a result of partnering with the local hospital. The merger between me and my beau was simple—I'd inherited everything. I'd added him to my phone line, as it was *convincingly* the right thing to do. Likewise, the utilities, internet, cable, insurance, and security system had all followed suit. This all seemed so normal to me, totally okay. It wasn't like I could go to my parents and ask them, "Should I be handling everything... paying for everything... responsible for everything?" There was no prototype for me to reference, no blueprint to follow. It was just me, my guy, his family, his way. Besides, my beau was this meagerly paid resident and I was this salaried pharmacist, or so he'd cleverly asserted. This way of doing things was *natural*. This was but a fleeting compromise for the greater good. An investment in *our* future. Such a plausible characterization. I went along with it.

When my beau had encouraged me to change certain ways of doing things, I'd espoused. This, too, I thought was compromise, part of being in a relationship, part of Operation Marriage. Take, for instance, laundry. There was nothing special about the way his mother did her laundry... she'd sort and wash them just as most of us do. There was, however, something special about the way her laundered clothes smelled. My guy just loved that smell ... "smelled like mama." He'd make such seemingly inconspicuous comments about this smell. In no time, I'd changed my laundry detergent and fabric softener to that which his mother used. And the way she'd folded towels made it so easy for them to fit in the linen closet. That, too, was an easy fix. I'd fold our towels the way his mother folded her towels. I even compromised Dolan's kitchen to meet my guy's standard. His mother's macaroni and cheese was thicker... she'd put *a pinch* of flour in it. And her chicken...her chicken was *crispier*, dipped in buttermilk then batter. I'd been championed to try her ways, and so I did. I thought this was all normal. Compromise. Part of becoming a good wife.

I was unknowingly becoming a distilled version of myself, being indoctrinated by my beau and his interestingly close family. His brother lived with their mother and his sister... only miles away. He and his mother, he and his siblings, and even he and his father spoke with one another daily, and often a number of times throughout the day. In the days that followed the closing, his mother, brother, and sister were given a key to our home. There was no discussion with the obvious other homeowner—no *Honey, what do you think?* or *Baby, are you cool with me giving our house key to three other people?* type conversation. There was just this unbeknownst to me issuance of keys... each of them given a key to *our* home and an open door policy along with it. His family would come and go freely, just as fluidly and as regularly as their multi-daily conversations. By no means coincidental on his part, we'd bought a home less than half a mile away from his mother's home, so there were the up close and personal conversations in lieu of the phone calls. Again, I thought this was all normal. Part of the Family Lessons 101 I'd missed somewhere between waking up to popcorn paint and going back and forth to my grandma's. My beau and his family ended every exchange with "I love you," and when his sister had told me, "I'll stab you if you ever hurt my brother," I took that too as a show of love. I'd grown up in a household that never quite used terms of endearment so I thought this way of life must be normal.

His family had made me feel like one of them... after all, I was *the* girl he'd brought home. I was *the* one. They'd seemingly accepted me for who I was—they'd accepted all of me. They'd accepted me in spite of my mother's mental illness and had accepted me in spite of my most skirted fears. I'd been transparent with my beau and his family, and for this, thought I'd earned their unwavering love. Even *our* phone calls with one another ended in "I love you." Their sweet spots had become *our* sweet spots. Their special places at the beach and vacation getaways had become *our* special places. We all worked at the same hospital, me, him, and his mother. We'd work together, eat dinner together, worship together, and repeat. This was my family. These people loved me. And this was normal.

Everything my guy asked of me outside of these things, the laundry, the cooking, the chores, surely had to be a compromise. Even as we moved through marriage counseling and my childhood minister tried to shed clarity on these not so normal things, I shunned them as mere compromise. Sadly, I'd confused my c's thanks to the camouflage of this so-called relationship. I'd mistaken compromise for what was inextricably the chameleon effect. I was more than just this distilled version of myself. I had become the version of me that my guy had wanted me to be. The version of me that was acceptable to him, acceptable to his family, acceptable for the vision he had created for his life. This whole thing was something far bigger than compromise.

Our wedding would prove to be no different. I'd envisioned a small church ceremony, but my guy was all pomp and circumstance. My fairytale ceremony, this intimate affair of family and friends, quickly exploded to a fanfare of more than a dozen groomsmen, bridesmaids, and guests galore. There was no budget, just my guy encouraging me to spend more money and me blindly doing so. What I didn't have the income to readily cover was paid for compliments of American Express, Chase, Capital One, and a few other generous creditors. My credit score was on point, so my guy's wish was my command. This too, he'd assured me, was but a fleeting compromise. "We will pay everything back in no time", so he said. And all the while, I thought this was what couples did... this was what partnership looked like... this was what love felt like.

My makeup was flawless. Every curl in place. Dress glistening. I'd remained as each bridesmaid filed out of the holding room of Paine College's Chapel. This was the place of my coronation, the footprint of my inception. I'd chosen this place because it reminded me of everything I once was not so very long ago. Now, here I stood, an almost unrecognizable version of myself. My bestie and matron of honor, LaShon, hugged me with an "I love you girl" as she glided out of the room. Renee and I had remained. I'd met Renee at one of the university's board review courses. She was sitting right behind me and had kept leaning forward to chat. I remember thinking, *Who is this chick?* On one of the breaks, Renee had moved from her seat to sit in my row in a seat right down from me. Her personality was striking. She was funny, witty, so free. Like so many of my classmates, Renee was also so very young (compared to those of us with undergraduate degrees). Though I'd only known her for a snippet of time, one thing for sure was this girl was not shy, a trait we'd both shared. By the time the review had come to an end, we'd exchanged contact information and vowed to keep in touch.

Now, here we were. As Renee and I approached the exit door at the end of the short hallway, I looked at her and said, "I am not supposed to do this." Renee laughed off my words, dismissed them as cold feet. She reminded me of all the guests, all the food, and all the money I'd spent. I'd always loved Renee's light-spirited personality, but in this moment, I was serious. Even firmer than the first time, I spoke, "I am not supposed to do this. I am not supposed to marry him." Renee casually locked her arm in mine and went into this soliloquy of all the many reasons why I would go forth with marrying this man. Renee's words grew muffled as I became lost in the white with gray vinyl composition tile, listening only to the clang of my heels against the sheen as I exited the door onto the pavement. There was a song, a prayer, poetry, another prayer, then our vows. In a matter of 45 minutes, I'd said yes to the unconscionable. Yet again, I'd said yes to not pursuing my own dreams, yes to tabling my own personal goals. Once more, I'd said yes to living our life his way, and yes to being okay with that. I'd said yes to a shit load of sheer shit!

At the age of 18, I'd ventured off from my family's church to do what my grandmother used to say, "Know God for yourself." My pastor used to pray this prayer right before delivering his message. Sunday after Sunday, he'd enter into his message with this adaptation from the Book of John. This prayer was pastor's way of communing with the Holy Spirit, willfully submitting to The most high. Pastor's prayer of supplication, paraphrased here, was simple: that *he* [pastor] might be decreased so that *He* [God] might be increased and His [God's] glory be made manifest. Over the next two years, I'd reflect heavily upon this invocation as I'd find myself not engaged in such an inveterate prayer yet ceremoniously being decreased so that he, my husband, might be increased.

My husband's family was rooted in Lodebar. His mother had been a nurse from the days of nurses making house calls. He'd shared stories with me of him and his older sister having camped out in the backseat of his mother's car as she worked and cared for her patients. His mother had cared for some of the who's who of Lodebar. This family was rooted in this community. I was now this appendage, joined to this family in holy matrimony but never to be mistaken as an original. In spite of my having my own credentials, I was regarded as *his* wife and *her* daughter-in-law… never my own person. He increased, I decreased. Back home, my family had become background noise as our visits to Augusta had grown fewer. Nevertheless, every time my grandmother saw my husband, she'd speak these words to him: "If you don't want her, bring her back." He'd stand before by grandmother with that darling, cunning smile, arms folded across his chest with his right hand in a soft fist, thumb nestled under his chin. He'd speak not a word in response to her statement... he'd only continue to smile that artificial smile and carry on. I'd never understood my grandmother's words, nor had I ever questioned her. But in what Dolan called "due time," God would surely reveal to me what my grandmother had already discerned.

The house was too quiet. There were four bedrooms, one turned office. There were the adult conversations that floated about the air of the kitchen, the same conversations that flitted across the dining room, the same conversations that would finally nestle in the living room. According to the husband, it was time. It was "time for the sound of pitter patter" throughout the house. Growing up with siblings can either make you feel one of two ways: you either grow up to be one of those people that wants to have kids of your own, or you don't. My brother, four years younger than me, was a total bad ass. I can easily recall the whoopings I'd been subjected to, just on his behalf ... he was exponentially terrible! Yet, in all his mischief, my brother was this source of so much of my joy. It was like the kid opened his eyes each morning and glanced around the universe for trouble. He was hilarious, all boy as *they* say (whoever they are), and not one for following directions. There was this one time we were at my grandmother's house playing with our cousins and some of the neighborhood kids. These were *the* days. Epic fun! My grandmother had laid out strict rules for each of us, and my brother was not to cross the street without me. So what do you know. This boy takes a mad 20-feet dash across the street anyway. Full speed ahead, oblivious to the oncoming car. And not only does he get disciplined for his actions, but so do I. Very disciplined and very publicly. Nevertheless, growing up with this amazing human being made me want children more than anything in the world. So when my husband spoke these words to me, I was all in. I stopped taking the pill and waited for life to happen.

❧

The Universe

We were having lunch with friends at this local family-owned café when it happened. I still feel the urge of pressure, pressure that I wanted to place my hand against and push back on but couldn't quite reach. That sort of pressure where you're trying to get out the word *wait* but can't. I jumped up from the table and bolted to the bathroom. My obstetrician had already told us what to expect. She'd searched for a heartbeat, and there was none. What should have been a developing embryo had halted, arrested in time. My world had likewise stopped. In my state of hysteria, my doctor had continued to explain what was to come. In the coming days to weeks, the products of conception would typically pass on their own. There would likely be no physical pain, maybe mild cramping, but lots of pressure. And there it was. Midday at lunch. Amongst great friends and good food, there was, to my dismay, pain. Not physical pain but emotional pain as I came to terms with exactly what my body was doing... purging. There was pressure, lots of pressure. And in this small bathroom for one, life happened and with it, the passing of the products of my misconception.

With loss comes change. Our second pregnancy had brought with it more loss, so change was inevitable. You'd think that this bodily purge would have presented me with this ideal opportunity to take pause, consult with the Universe, assume a position of total surrender, seated with Mother

Earth, face open to the sun and hands as well, palms facing upward. You'd think this was that ah-ha moment for me to figure out what the hell was going on. With each purge, I was losing so much more of self, an absolute I'd painstakingly identified yet knew not how to respond to. I'd blamed myself for the loss of our pregnancies, an onus my husband was more than happy to allow me to assume. There was no processing the pain, no understanding, no appreciation for what the Universe may have been trying to interject. There was me assuming responsibility for my body's rejection, and there was me trying to make things right through more compromise. So this magnanimous version of change reared its head in the form of what my husband had colorfully named a "cocaine white" Audi S5 Coupe. He'd so badly wanted a new car, devoted time on end to building this car on line to his exact specifications, sharing this dream car concept with his brother and best friend. He'd even been in contact with one of the local dealerships, asking the lead salesman to keep an eye out for this particular color, make, and model. So when this "cocaine white" 2008 Audi S5 Coupe came up for sale nearly 400 miles away on the sunny coast of Sarasota, Florida, my downtrodden heart leaped at the opportunity to buy my husband this car and fix what I'd thought was my private ineptitude.

When the Universe speaks, it's wise to listen. Be still. Silence the distractions. Listen. The Universe was speaking, only I couldn't hear her. My husband had told me "There's something wrong with you." We could get pregnant, but I couldn't stay pregnant. Something was wrong with me... The volume of his words had made me tone deaf to the Universe. While she was saying *Not Now! Not Him!*, I was distracted. Distracted by the agony of his words and the brokenness of my womb. The Universe was speaking, but my spirit was in turmoil, spiraling in motion to right this wrong and bare for this man a child. There was no time to be still, or so I reasoned. There were tests to be run, options to weigh, a means to fix whatever was *wrong with me.*

My OB had ordered a battery of tests, the earliest of which spoke to the life already growing inside of me. She'd quickly started hormone replacement therapy to support the developing embryo. I went to nearly each appointment alone, and though trepidation joined me on the table, joy rushed right in with the visibility of movement and the sound of a strongly beating heart. All the while, I'd become pretty good at this thing of not listening to the Universe. There was the physical act of going to church, the ritual of prayer, reverence for a higher power. But somehow, I'd become disconnected from my power source. The morning of January 25, 2010, the Universe spoke. My body felt unlike that of my own, and a small voice beckoned for me to stay at home, rest. I was the workhorse of our marriage, however, so there was no time for rest. There were bills to be paid, the mortgage, and other added expenses right down to the landscaping, so there was no time to stay at home. I dismissed the nudge and reported for my twelve-hour shift. A few hours later, I'd find myself in labor and delivery, fully immersed in preterm labor.

The following morning, me and all my brokenness sighed breaths of relief and tears of passion as I gave birth to a 5lb 9oz baby boy. He was five weeks early but healthy and absolutely beautiful. His name was to be Isaiah, honoring the salvation of the Lord. Yet, once again, there was compromise. The birth of my son gave life to the first grandchild, a celebration that would be short lived as my sister-in-law arrived at the hospital with an announcement of her own. She was pregnant. On the heels of a birth that paid homage to both life and loss for me, my husband's sister had announced that she was pregnant. With a fleeting partner on the horizon, my sister-in-law would now move back home, and my husband had made it clear that *we* would help her. Though he was a resident with a meager income, *we* would help her. He'd made it clear, crystal clear, that her child was to be afforded the same way of life as our son, with no expenses spared. I, the compromising chameleon, conceded.

Mothering was this fun, adventurous, and yes, sometimes tiring thing for me. Miles away from my own family, I'd adopted a local group of mothers as my extended family. We'd meet once a month at a local church for fellowship, prayer, support, and camaraderie. Grounded in faith and rooted in a mutual love for life, this group helped to shape the fortitude of my mothering. With this group of phenomenal women, I learned the magic of the slow cooker (something that Dollie did not have) and the importance of creating "me time." With me as a working mom fettered to a husband that was routinely missing in action, these tools were pivotal to my daily success. I'd restructured my time management and found my own way. From bath time to breakfast, daycare pick up to morning drop offs, it was me and my son. Each day with my son was a glimpse into Mother Nature's infinite majesty. He was the physical manifestation of my soul in motion. He was my life.

The introduction of a child into a relationship can either strengthen the unity partners share or give way to turbulence in an already unsettling climate. The birth of my son was silence to all the distractions, realignment with the Universe. I was a wife, I was a mom, I was a friend, I was a hard worker, I was busy, and I was often times tired… but, I wasn't stupid. The more I was tasked with, the more awakened I'd become. As all of the artifices of *compromise* and all of the noise of *us being a team* had begun to fade away, things had indeed become clearer. I was in something far more convoluted than marriage. I was single parenting, all the while tethered to this person, a relationship likened to a handmaid and her commander. With each day, I'd grown more and more emotionally exhausted and even more so detached. With my husband-turned-commander, there was always lip service and *reasoning*, both semantics for lies filled only with more empty promises, softly decorated with words of affirmation. To impugn my husband, however, was to be met with swift reprimand, an admonishment that tarried like the sweet mint gum found on his breath. He'd found utility in disagreements and seized these opportunities to emotionally eviscerate me. Whatever *this* was, I'd not signed up for it. I was deadlifting our family, fatigued in lockout. It was time to let go of the dead weight. The Universe was speaking. My spirit was still, and I was listening. If I were going to do this alone, I would go it alone.

"I want a divorce." My words were that simple; his declination, not so much. I was many shades of "crazy" and much more simply "nothing," viscously pummeled by the words of the good doctor. Seething with anger and basking in the fullness of his self-righteousness and sheer arrogance, my husband laughed at the notion of me *trying* to divorce him, all the while hurling more and more painful insults. He and his over inflated ego had arrived. The pain of my mother was woven into this unconscionable tapestry, embroidered with loss, every known conceivable hurt, and the ostentatious threat of never seeing my son again. The opening act was done, and the headliner had definitely taken center stage. My husband's true self had arrived. The role-playing had been put to rest, and his arrogance and self-righteousness was on full display. His words were weighted, deliberate, heartless, and cold. He'd meant every single word. It is said that where there is smoke, there is fire. And a full flame had erupted before me. Defeated and afraid, I cowered, retreating into the very dead space of my marriage.

It was the year end residency banquet, and my husband, chief resident, was up to speak. Living out his second career choice, the great actor had taken the podium. With a tearful voice, he thanked me for "doing all the heavy lifting," for being his "supportive wife," and for being a "wonderful mother." Any other time, I would have believed him. I would have joined the audience with their endearing sighs. I would have welcomed his mother's gentle touch on my right hand. Any other time, the shrewd ways of my husband would have gone unnoticed. But this particular evening, all dressed up in my after six attire, and pregnant with our second child, his carefully engineered words were repugnant and had fallen on more than deafened ears. Here we were, the picture perfect family. We'd been featured in the local paper, cast as the happy family everyone had thought us to be. I was the doctor's wife, our child was the doctor's son, and this child that I now carried would surely follow suit in this characterization that spoke nothing of self but everything of ownership, attachment, and property. We were our own little small town dynasty, only I had threatened to disgrace the good doctor's brand in filing for a divorce. He'd given me the opportunity "to straighten up," "get my act together." My abject capitulation to such orders, however, would prove more than simply unsettling.

I'd willingly given my husband my life, happily given *to* him *life*, freely shared with him everything. Yet here I sat, listening to this bullshit ass speech, suborned by deceit, enveloped in fear, crippled by the threats of never seeing my children again. There were so many misguided fears surrounding my already pregnant universe. *Leave* was the word that resonated in my spirit overshadowed by *but*. *But* there were so many unknowns. My husband had encouraged me to pursue part-time work "in the interest of our family," so the one thing he'd governed was the insurance. Pregnant with no insurance??? Then, there was the need for "more space to accommodate our growing family," so we'd upgraded our home to this more than 4,000 square foot monstrosity, financed solely in my name.

Bankruptcy??? I was pregnant, isolated, afraid, worn. Where would I go? Who'd understand? Who'd possibly understand a pregnant woman leaving her husband, this revered doctor, this pillar of the community? Who'd understand all the control, all the rules, all the compromises? There was just so much to figure out - all variables Monday morning quarterbacking would prove plausible but sadly dead on the play.

As my husband's mother's touch jolted through my right hand, the Universe carefully seated herself at my left hand, unveiling the dubious nature of husband's subterfuge. As he continued to speak, so did She. The Universe recalled each argument, each one with more volume, more hurt, and more intensity than the last. As my husband floated his words like feathers through the air, the Universe reminded me of the weight of his physical touch, when words alone weren't quite enough. As he wooed the audience with the magic of his charisma, the Universe replayed each coax to compromise, outlining all that had been taken and all that had been lost, including self. A great friend had once told me that when a person shows you who they really are, you should believe them. The man at the podium, the man center stage, the charming guy with the flashy smile and soft dimples, the homegrown, good doctor. There stood my private hell, my personal nightmare, my unyielding fate. His words, merciful lies. His disposition, fake. He was an impostor. A con artist. All of it, an act. This well thought-out stage play, put on for an audience of one. My husband's family was nothing more than co-conspirators, helping to advance his agenda. And me, a fool, complicit in my own detriment. Only this time, I'd had enough, one word that would soon come to be met with the full force of my husband's discipline, craft, and malfeasance.

❧

Enough

Wednesday, August 14, 2013. The alarm sounded at 6:30 a.m., and my day had began as usual … coffee, get dressed, get the kids up, dressed, and fed, then out the door, off to daycare. With work not for several hours, I head to the gym. I then run errands, wash my car, and have lunch with one of my best girlfriends. Slightly before 2:00 p.m., I clock in for a short shift of only four hours. Then, off to get my two sons from daycare and home to resume my fulltime commitment as mom and wife. Late night, children upstairs in bed, then in comes the husband. Late, with the usual rhetoric of "I was seeing patients," with a sprinkle of "clinic ran late," and topped with "I was dictating charts." A heated argument ensues. The good doctor's penchant for getting home late was ancient old and was way past tired. There was always this *reasonable explanation* for his never getting home before 9:00 p.m. with a hospital-owned clinic that closed at 5:00 p.m. And when the *reasonable explanation* didn't go over quite so well, he'd exclaim, "Remember, I told you I'd be late," followed by how the responsibility of our three-year-old and one-year-old was making me "forgetful" and "overwhelmed." My husband would attempt to explain away everything.

This night, however, the Universe had arrived hours ahead of my lying husband. She'd reminded me to stay focused and steer clear of his unaccountability. There was the whisper, *Enough.* Enough with my husband's control. Enough with his mind games. Enough with all the fighting and false personas. Enough with my compromising while he remained this irresponsible post in our marriage. Enough with his being this placeholder. Enough with my constant decrease, his constant increase. Enough with what my husband had called "all the heavy lifting." With all this "heavy lifting," my muscle memory was on fleek and quite frankly, done with this exhaustive workout of a marriage. I'd had ENOUGH! For the umpteenth time, I'd reminded my husband that I was "unhappy with this so-called marriage," and for the fourth time, I'd demanded a divorce! Moments later, I popped an alprazolam, brown-girl-angry-stormed off to my bedroom, and retired for bed, alone, as usual. What seemed like hours later, I recall my husband shaking me "to talk," but I could not engage and continued to sleep.

W.T.F.

Thursday, August 15, 2013. Around 7:00 a.m., I'd awakened, once again, to being shaken. Not only is it 7:00 a.m. and my husband is still at home, but he's fully dressed, explains he's "called out of work," and is taking our sons to daycare, all of which is totally bizarre. He tells me to get dressed as "we're going to see a marriage counselor … we have an appointment." Married now for five years and having asked for a divorce four times, I believe my husband to have finally gotten the message. So I get up from bed, notify work that I won't be in today, and get dressed for this "appointment." I put on one of my best outfits, a green, blue and white vertical-lined maxi dress accented by three-inch green wedges. Oh, how much I would grow to detest this outfit later.

Around 10:30 a.m., in the car and on our merry way, I began to ask questions like, "Where are we going?", "Where is our appointment?", "What time is our appointment?", and "Who's the counselor?" As I'm knee-deep texting my cousin making plans for a much awaited weekend trip home to Augusta, my husband starts by telling me we're "going to Valdosta to see a psychiatrist." *What the fuck?!* was the best response my brain could reckon, along with a million other expletives. Every imaginable thought bolted through my brain at record speed. Surely, this was a joke.

We're approaching one of the main exits in Lodebar, when my husband tells me, "I'm taking you to the emergency room to get some help." Nearly at the point of throwing up, shaking and hyperventilating, I can't help but listen as my husband continues to tell me this warped story of how I'd told him, the night prior, that I wanted to kill myself. My brain implodes! I am now in a full panic attack. I am in imminent danger. Realizing the seriousness in his face with his words echoing in my gut, I began to beg him to take the next exit and take me to my primary care doctor's office. Minutes later, we were in the parking lot of my doctor's office. My husband instructed me to remain in the car while he went inside to speak with my doctor. Physically, I remain, but my thoughts are fleeting with terror and my heart is pounding through my chest. My hands are shaking. I try to calm down. This was the flight-or-fight response that flooded my body when hit by the man that supposedly loved me. This was the jolt that raced through my body when an argument suddenly turned into a real life chokehold with my face planted flush with the wall. This feeling … this was the anxious chaos of flight-*and*-flight intermixed…the feeling of my body losing all control. The feeling of my body not knowing, under no certain terms, what to do. This feeling was fear. Little did I know, sitting in this fear would command the rest of my life.

Dr. Smith, approaches the passenger side door with my husband. My heart is pounding at the base of my ears…my hands are clammy…sweat is now beading from the lines of my scalp, the creases of my thighs, the folds behind my knees. I can hear the glob of spit sliding down my throat as Dr. Smith echoes my husband's sentiments, directing me to "Go see the doctor in Valdosta." The expression on his face was even more disconcerting. Overcome by all of this happening at once—the lies, the coercion, the uncertainty of what exactly had happened that morning with my sons—I began to cry. I was afraid. Scared. Trapped. Isolated. Alone. Betrayed. And not only had I been lied to but lied on. Again, I sat there. Paralyzed with fear. I spoke not a word but sat there, in a state of shock, likened only to the moment that I'd realized I was being raped. Motionless…quiet…uncontrollable tears. My core said, RUN! Open the damn door and RUN! Yet I found myself frozen, knowing that the inability to move sealed my fate. Nevertheless, there I sat as my husband proceeded to drive in a direction that was totally foreign to me. I had no idea where my phone was and no idea where my white Beamer would finally come to a stop. After driving quite some ways, my husband nonchalantly pulls into a drive-thru and begins to order. Gripped with gut wrenching pain, I continued to sob, face buried in the passenger window. Out of nowhere, my husband instructs me to drink from the paper cup he was moving in my direction, to "*help me calm down.*" I drank from the cup. In mere minutes, I felt overcome with sleepiness and passed out.

Where am I?

W *here am I?!* This is the first thought that flooded my groggy brain. My husband was trying to get me out of the car. My head was foggy, thoughts cloudy, judgment impaired. With shoulders interlocked, as you would be with a drunken buddy, my husband walked me to what was a hospital entrance. Inside, he sat me in a chair in the waiting area as he went to speak with the woman sitting behind the desk. I still could not comprehend what was happening … no matter how hard I tried to put the puzzle together, it was as though it remained scattered on the floor. Convoluted thoughts came to mind like, *You're smart! Get up and get out of here! Something is wrong! Think! You know something's wrong here! Get up now!* Yet, I was stuck. During my time as a research apprentice, I'd studied a phenomenon experienced by some stroke patients called dysphasia. It's that time period following damage to the brain where the patient may have difficulty using or comprehending speech. Here I sat, as a physically, emotionally, and mentally sound individual, unable to utter a single word. I wanted to talk, wanted to scream, wanted to bellow out "HELP ME," yet couldn't. All I could think is *Where am I? What is happening?* and *Why is he (my husband) doing this to me?*

ॐ

Triage

Moments later, my husband returns to me in the waiting room. Once again, interlocked, we move in the direction of a nurse standing at an opened door. The nurse begins to ask me a series of questions, all of which are answered by my caring husband, the doting doctor. My vitals are taken, and I am moved into a patient room with my husband at bedside and nurse stationed outside my door. My wedged shoes are removed, and I am given a pair of white socks with which to garb my feet. Dozing in and out of consciousness, I see a doctor enter my room. This doctor introduces himself, shaking hands with my husband (who has introduced himself as *Doctor...*), and the dialogue begins. With a gentle head nod, my husband steers the conversation outside of my room. Soon after, the doctor returns to my bedside and begins to ask me about this *plan* to kill myself. He asks about these "extreme highs and lows" I'd reportedly been having, and he asks about my "wanting to be run over by a train." As I listen to the words floating from his mouth, my thoughts begin to form. I verbally and vehemently deny the accusation and silently think –*You've got to be fucking kidding me?! First of all, the thought of killing myself ... really?! I just want to divorce this asshole! Secondly, let's just be realistic for a moment ... I am a pharmacist with unlimited access to medications ... IF (and that's a huge fucking IF) I were ever to contemplate such life ending thoughts, I'm sure I could do far better than a* *damn train, you stupid idiot ... just listen to how asinine the words sound coming from your mouth. Hell, I'd have to figure out where the nearest train tracks are, drive myself to those tracks, lie down on the tracks, and then just patiently wait for a fucking train to come along ... not to mention all the passersby that would likely interrupt my serene lying-in-wait. Really?!* – This moment was so surreal, like the out-of-body, dramatic, wishful thinking animations flocking the television series "Ally McBeal." Except this was very real. These accusations, very real. All lies but nonetheless very real. My thoughts were interrupted by the doctor continuing with, "You know what this means ... I have to hold you here."

Ten Thirteen

urled up in a fetal position, I laid there in that bed
sobbing. The doctor explained to me that I was being
"involuntarily committed," what is known as a 1013.
My husband stood bedside with his arms folded across his
body and the most beautiful solemn smirk upon his face.
Several healthcare professionals came in and out of the room,
all reiterating the necessity of the 1013 and outlining the events
to now follow. Stripped of all my belongings and donned with
a medical wristband, I was ushered into the backseat of a
police car and transported to what would be my dwelling place
for the next few days. I gazed out the back window of the police
car to see my husband happily trailing the car as I was taken
to yet another unknown. There are no words to explain the
gamut of emotions that scourged through my psyche. I was
in mental, emotional, and physical pain. I'd cried so much
that my inner core sobbed while my outer parts sat composed.

Pain mixed with anger is a cocktail for redemption. For the
previous eight years, I'd been an amazing partner to the man
that had now blatantly lied to me, lied about me, and lied on
me. I'd carried the financial burden of the household while my
husband completed medical school and residency. As mother
to two amazing sons, I'd unselfishly sacrificed advancing my
career to take the stage as part-time pharmacist and full-time
parent. I'd been front and center at every ceremony, smiled
and conversed at every social event, and fought back the tears

when denied trips to go home and visit with family. I'd shown up in a marriage that was a mirage. And here I was ... in this real moment... and no matter how I ran the numbers, replayed the years in my head, all the brains, love, support, and sacrifice had somehow equated to this 1013.

Greenleaf

The car came to a stop. The officer took a single step to the driver's side back door, opened it, and I stepped out. I still remember the puddles on the broken pavement as I hurdled around them, careful not to wet my white socks. In a matter of minutes, muddled with lies, the culmination of my life had come to fruition. My hard work, years of discipline, zeal for life, all lost in this moment. Here I stood. Age 32. Mother of two. Pharmacist, friend, believer. My husband and this manufactured state of insanity. Here I stood. Me and these white socks. With a couple of taps on a steel door, a man appeared welcoming me inside. He asked if I wanted to say goodbye to my husband, and I answered by proceeding to walk inside. The officer followed suit, handing the man some paperwork and the bag of my belongings, and engaging in their notably so-routine patient transfer report. I was seated next to a disheveled patient as the intake process began.

Quickly moved through a series of secured doors, I was taken to the sector that would now be my residence. As protocol, I was asked a series of questions, including what became my favorite one, "Why are you here?" The now, less inhibited version of myself informed each staff member that I was there because my husband had lied … because he was a narcissist and was angry at my intentions to file for divorce. My body was stripped of its clothes and searched, my cavities inspected. It was the second most intrusive experience of my life. I felt greater than violated, more than demeaned. There was nothing to do but wait until the procedural examination was over.

With my dress back on, I met my intake counselor. He welcomed me to Greenleaf Behavioral Health Hospital. The counselor explained the purpose and goals of the inpatient program and outlined what would be my day-to-day schedule. This outline included when meals would be served, group therapy sessions would take place, phone calls would be permitted, and what "lights out" entailed. What for some would serve as their place of healing and restoration was now my prison. In a matter of minutes, I'd lost my freedom, my rights over my body, my rights. Period. I faded in and out of the meeting pondering *Where are my sons? ... What has* he *told them? ... Are they afraid? ... Are they wondering why Mommy didn't pick them up from daycare today?* ... and the thoughts continued. My private conversation was interrupted by the counselor telling me which psychiatrist I'd been assigned and asking me if there were any questions. I sat quietly thinking, *Today is Thursday.* This will all be over soon. I will be home Sunday, maybe even in time for church. Nope, no questions.

Reality set in. I found myself in an inpatient psychiatric facility with some of my very own patients. I knew their stories, respected their individual journeys, yet our disposition was not the same. I was initially set to board with a patient I'd directly cared for only days earlier but was more than pleased when the staff informed me that I would be given a private quarter. I was thankful for the solitude that this 14 x 13 foot space would offer. I needed this sanctuary to process the events of the day and comb through the nefarious developments of the night before. This meditation, however, would have to wait. It was almost dinnertime, a mandatory event, and I needed to speak with my children before phone time had come to an end. I called my sons, only to get my husband's voicemail. I dialed his number, each time with a greater sense of urgency than the last. I stood at the makeshift phone booth—blindly staring at the other two phones stationed to my right—thinking surely my husband had come to terms with the gravity of his *mistake* ... surely he would answer and offer up a million apologies for the error of his ways. I called over, and over, and over again. Yet the end result was still the same. Voicemail. Voicemail. I had been completely cut off ... cut off from my reality ... cut off from my sons ... involuntarily disconnected. I held the phone to my chest and sobbed. Then, I began to dial my brother.

My brother, though the younger of the two of us, had always been a calming, reassuring, motivational force in my life. In his usual candor, he reminded me to stay calm and to know that everything would be okay. My brother had no knowledge of the sick events that had led to my being at Greenleaf, a position I would soon come to learn was universal as I reached out to other family and one of my closest friends. This revelation would have to wait. My phone calls were interrupted by the call for mandatory group therapy sessions.

❧

Day 2

F riday, August 16, 2013. I awakened to find myself trapped in a very real nightmare. Indeed, I was at Greenleaf Behavioral Health Hospital. Indeed, I had been committed. Indeed, I had been involuntarily institutionalized. This was real. I lay there in my twin size bed, staring at the ceiling... there were no answers there. I slowly turned my head to the left, wet eyes landing on the vacant twin size bed only feet away from mine... still, no answers. I looked over the room, to the pine door, to the dresser chest, to the open door leading to my private bathroom... still, no answers. No answers to the flurry of thoughts racing through my brain. A complete thought couldn't exit before another one had already barged in. I cried that cry where there's no sound... no motion... no effort, just tears that escape your eyes. For the life of me, I could not understand why... why this, why me, why now... why. I'd rested peacefully through the night, better sleep than I'd had in years. So even in the midst of my sadness, my thoughts were coherent, yet all the while bewildered. I planted my white socks on the floor, stood to my feet, wiped my face, dragging snot from cheek to cheek, and made a valiant effort to get myself together (whatever the hell that now meant).

Still wearing my maxi dress, I left my room on this mission to get answers. There were only small windows of time afforded to using the phone, so there I would start. I called my husband's cell phone. Again, no answer. I took notice of the time and decided to call his clinic. On the receiving end of that call was a familiar, pleasant, welcoming voice. It was Cora, my husband's scheduler, and it was evident from her usual cheerful conversation that she'd had no knowledge of the heinous events that had transpired in my universe. In typical fashion, Cora asked about the kids and continued the conversation as was customary. When I asked, however, to speak with the good doctor, Cora's tone quickly changed to one of bafflement. She answered, "I'm sorry but he's not here… he'd taken today and the coming week off months ago." Cora's words drifted as the phone slid down my now wet cheek. I never even placed the phone back on the receiver as my shattered self was in too great of a hurry to return to the privacy of my room. This—the lies, Greenleaf, all of it—was planned. This had all been a sick, well thought out, calculated plan. All of it! Just one huge, hate-filled, seamlessly orchestrated, immensely fucked up plan.

Where is this God?

W e all believe in something or someone. As early as I can remember, my grandmother, the wife of a Baptist minister, had instilled in me the principles of faith, even in the midst of the unknown. Every aspect of my life had been built around this concept of God. There was church every Sunday morning, starting with Sunday school and often spanning regular service plus a program at our own church or a neighboring church. I was an usher in the church and sometimes sang with the choir, for in my grandmother's eyes, "an idle mind was the devil's workshop." There was weeknight service, Vacation Bible School. There was scripture quoted after communal prayer, and there was family prayer to bring in each new year together. There were times when we'd simply talk about what my grandmother would refer to as "The Goodness of the Lord," those hard times that I was too young and inexperienced to appreciate but nevertheless, loved to share in with her. Sometimes, I'd struggle with this thing called faith, one such struggle that led me on my own path at the age of 18. I'd grapple with *why* then I'd wrestle with *why not*. But with the faintest show of emotion, my grandmother would tell me, "Just keep on livin'… you'll understand by and by."

Even with the passing of her husband, I'd witnessed this strong woman brave the storms of caring for her children and even her children's children. And when the Universe had asked for the return of her children in death, my grandmother had remained stoic and humbly obliged, all the while still praising this God—this God she'd taught me to revere, this God she'd assured me would sustain. I'd watched my grandmother glorify this God as she hand-stitched the holes in her undergarments, just so that she could save the money it would cost to buy new ones, and continue to provide for her family. I meditated on these things as I sat in mandatory group session, still mortified by the course of events that had led to a permanent imprint on my life. I thought of all the teachings, countless miracles proclaimed in the Bible, and I could not help but think, *Where is this God?* My soul was broken. No prayer, no fond memory, no person could assuage the agonizing pain. I sat there, deaf to the words coming from the group leader's mouth, lost in time and space, thinking, *God, where are you? How could you allow this to happen? How could you allow this to happen to me? Why?*

It was on day two that I believe this God of my grandparents showed up at Greenleaf and delivered me from my darkest hours. No, God didn't just swoop in with a magic wand and make everything reset. And as badly as I'd wanted him to, God didn't teleport through the walls of Greenleaf, snatch me up, and return me to the sons I'd been taken from. What He did, however, was far greater. God mended wounds not visible to the naked eye and exonerated my weary soul. I've discovered that, sometimes, His mercy shows up in people, places, time, intangibles, all of which I experienced at Greenleaf. It was on the morning of this second day that I noticed a Holy Bible resting on a small accent table adjacent to the telephone booth. It was as if this Book screamed my name in a silence that only I could hear. I still remember standing there, staring down at this Book as though I'd never seen one before. I was on my way to breakfast, another mandatory gathering, so I decided to grab it up and take it with me.

After breakfast, before the first group session of the day, I pulled a chair to a nearby window in the lobby and opened the Bible. All the years I'd spent growing up in church—ushering, attending Sunday school and seasonal revivals, reciting scripture on program—had not prepared me for this very moment. I sat there, glaring down at my white socks, holding a Book that now seemed so foreign to me. I didn't know what scripture to read that would make sense of all the madness … which verse would bare a sense of peace. It was then that I heard a still, small voice direct me to the Book of Psalms. In the quiet of that early morning, I read and wept.

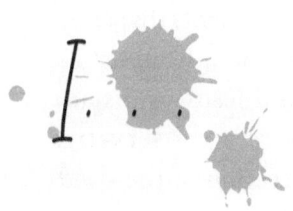

That afternoon in group, I tuned in as the group leader explained this fundamental concept known as "I" statements. "I" statements or "I" messages are designed to appropriately assign accountability between the speaker and listener. This concept was developed in the 1960s by Dr. Thomas Gordon, a clinical psychologist who's widely recognized as a pioneer in teaching communication skills and conflict resolution.[2] "I" statements focus on the feelings or beliefs of the speaker as opposed to the thoughts and characteristics the speaker attributes to the listener.[3] Simply put, "I" statements are about me (the speaker in this context) and how I feel or what I believe about me. As I listened to the group leader, I became empowered by this concept and began to apply these "I" statements to my own life.

Having grown up in church, I could not help but think back to scripture and the numerous "I" statements laced throughout. The beauty of statements like "I am the Alpha and Omega" (Revelation 1:8), "I am the way, and the truth, and the life" (John 14:6), or "I AM WHO I AM" (Exodus 3:14) sent rays of courage through my spirit. I meditated on the power underlying these statements and the power beheld by the speaker. I thought that since I am a child of God, I too have this boldness to declare "I" over my life. This is my life! My story! I am the narrator of this story, and as grim as it may seem…as impossible as it may appear, I still have a fighting chance.

The most profound of the biblical "I" statements that came to mind was that from the Gospel of Matthew, Chapter 22. Starting at the twenty-third verse, we find Jesus in dispute with the Sadducees. The Sadducees were a conservative Jewish sect that did not believe in resurrection of the dead. In this encounter, the Sadducees challenge Jesus on one of the teachings of Moses, marriage at the resurrection. This teaching held that if a man and woman were wed, without children, and the man died, then that man's brother was to marry the widow and raise up offspring in honor of the deceased. In this argument, seven brothers were proposed to marry this widow. The Sadducees then pose the question to Jesus: "Now then, at the resurrection, whose wife will she be of the seven, since all of them were married to her?" (Matthew 22:28) Jesus corrected the Sadducees for their ignorance in the Word and answered, in summary, "I am the God of Abraham, the God of Isaac, and the God of Jacob?" (Matthew 22:32) Simply put, Jesus checked the Sadducees, stating, "You are in error because you do not know the Scriptures or the power of God." (Matthew 22:29)

The power in this "I" statement rests in knowing the covenant that God had made with Abraham and his descendants. As I sat in group, I reflected on this covenant that God had promised to deliver His people and bring them into the Promised Land (Genesis 12, 15, 17). I silently celebrated this intimate moment, recognizing that I am a child of God and knowing that I too would be delivered! Though I didn't know when, and I sure as hell didn't know how, I knew, for sure, that deliverance was already on its way. Greenleaf was but for a moment. I left that group with more grit than I'd walked in with. I began to speak words of affirmation over my life like: "I am not crazy!" "I am fearfully and wonderfully made." "I am a child of the most high God and because He Is, I Am!" "I am strong, a force to be reckoned with!" "This shit hurts! But I can handle it!" And "I don't want to, but I Can do this!"

Ten Fourteen

The joy experienced in my group session was short lived, met with a shocking blow of disappointment in my individual session. My assigned inpatient psychiatrist started our so-called interview by telling me he had spoken at length with my husband. A man I'd known for a mere hour was now prepared to *diagnose me* ... a thought that resounded in my mind. There was no comprehensive evaluation of my medical history, no dialogue with my primary care provider or other healthcare providers, no detailed clinical interview, no behavior inventory, no Mood Disorder Questionnaire, no diagnostic assessment, no nothing. There was just this lie and the scurrilous charge birthed from it.

I listened as this psychiatrist shared with me, at random, the story of a young Haitian girl that would venture door to door, engaging in sexual activities with the men of her village. I listened to this uncanny story thinking *what the hell does this have to do with me*, and *why the hell are you telling me this?* Finally, I questioned the doctor's need to tell me this story, but he compelled me to listen. I felt more than uncomfortable as this psychiatrist continued to describe the young girl's capricious behaviors. When he brought the story to a close, he began to ask me questions about my own sexual preferences, questions I'd found not only inappropriate but equally extraneous.

As this doctor continued to speak, I allowed my thoughts to wander. Looking through this lens, I thought of my husband.

I thought of words like *morals, truth, integrity.* I thought about the oath my husband had taken as a medical doctor. I thought about his *immoral* behavior ... I thought about his *lies.* One of the core precepts of the oath taken by medical doctors is *primum non nocere,* the Latin phrase meaning "first, do no harm." I thought about these words as this doctor's tangential singular conversation ensued. Though I was not even his [my husband's] patient, my husband had definitely caused harm. His actions, however convincing, were not out of his good faith to "help me." This wasn't some saving grace, some heroic act on the good doctor's behalf to intercept a threat that had never existed. My husband was not this Good Samaritan. This was no *Captain Save Her* rescue mission. There was no suicidal ideation, no plan, no intent. Just divorce. And this, this was everything but "help"! This was harm, in its purest form, handed down by my husband.

My grandmother used to say this prayer where she'd thank God for waking her up, "clothed in" her "right mind." I thought of her as I tuned back in to this stranger. I was definitely woke and definitely in my right mind. So there was absolutely no receiving his "diagnosis" and no need to engage this ill-informed individual . My refusal to accept my one-hour-all-in psychiatrist's diagnosis had not only vexed him but resulted in longer imprisonment. Because I'd challenged his ability to label me based on the false narrative of another individual, the 1013 was escalated to a 1014. I didn't even know what the hell this meant, but the doctor was all too happy to inform me of its meaning. My objection had earned me an involuntary five-day committal, and this doctor was prepared to further extend my length of stay so long as I "continued to not cooperate," so much so that I could be a "ward of the state." Time stopped. The room began to spin. My heart was pounding out of my chest. All I could think of were my kids.

Memories of my sons playing their drum set and shooting Little Tikes® basketball zipped through my brain. I could not breathe.

Dr. Martin Luther King once said, "Let no man pull you so low as to hate him".[4] So instead of allowing hatred for my husband and current situation to infiltrate my being and dictate my fate, I chose to control my own narrative! I chose to be present in the moment ... to actually listen to the stories of the amazing people surrounding me ... to bury the pain and agony of my own journey and pour out love to those in need. Only God could deliver me from my hurt, but I sure as hell could try and love on and encourage those around me. From my previous failed attempts to fix a narcissist, I'd learned how I give and receive love, lessons garnered from Gary Chapman's book *The 5 Love Languages: The Secret to the Love that Lasts*.[5] My love language was gift giving. I demonstrate love by giving tangible and sometimes intangible gifts to others. Who would have ever imagined that *love* could be translated as an "extreme high"? Nevertheless, I chose to now let my crazy be contagious! I chose to continue to love, a decision that redefined the course of my incarceration at Greenleaf and the journey that lie ahead.

Instead of checking out during group and venturing to another time and place when engaged in conversation, I listened. With my whole heart and mind, I listened. I listened to the journey of individuals struggling with things like clinical depression, anxiety disorder, post traumatic stress disorder, body acceptance, and anger management. I felt the heart of their tears. I could relate to their pain and grasp the fullness of their anger. The assault on my character was seemingly minute as I now listened to the stories of those that had been battling for some time and others that had just involuntarily joined the fight. I would later come to appreciate that these brave men and women were engaged in what author Brené Brown regards as "daring greatly".[6] These amazing men and women had the courage to step into the arena, true grit to press on, and the audacity to believe that there was something greater on the other side. They inspired me to own my story, in spite of the fact that someone else had attempted to script it for me. For the first time in my life, I took off the armor of independence, ambition, and success. Cloaked only in my three days worn, musty maxi dress and dingy white socks, I too stepped into the arena.

That arena took me on a journey back to my youth. Growing up as kids in downtown Augusta, my grandmother would sometimes take me and my cousins on store runs with her to places like H. L. Green and Gurley's Supermarket. These stores were the hallmarks of their time. My cousins and I loved piling up in the backseat of my grandmother's car and going to the store. Once we'd pulled into the parking lot, my grandmother would begin this speech that we all knew by heart. "Don't touch nothing!" she'd say. She'd continue by saying, "Taking what don't belong to you is stealing." These words resonated in my mind as I sat in room 126 at Greenleaf, staring down at my dirty white socks. I could hear the words of my grandmother echo in my spirit as I gazed at the soft brown outline now taking shape as the form of my feet wearing through the white socks. According to Dolan Hudson, stealing was simply taking what didn't belong to you, a definition parallel to that found in the dictionary. The verb *steal* is further defined as "to take (the property of another or others) without permission or right, especially secretly or by force".[7] Those that engage in the deleterious act of stealing are commonly known as thieves and the act they commit as theft.

In spite of my grandmother's teachings, I'd once found myself straddling the backseat of a police car. At the age of 11, my mother had decided to take what didn't belong to her. She'd waltzed through Kmart, picking up body spray fragrances, jewelry, and other garments, blatantly shoving these items into her bra, oversized purse, and even a bag she'd lifted while perusing the store. Psychologically imbalanced, my mother didn't care who'd seen her stealing. She'd given no weight to the magnitude of her actions or the repercussions. She didn't lend a care to the little girl, her own daughter, that was with her. We'd exited Kmart, followed by two men that were notably security guards. They called out, "Ma'am." My mother continued to stroll along, seemingly oblivious to the men's existence. As she pulled items from her bra and placed the bags in the trunk of our red Ford Tempo, I pleaded for her to stop. The security guards had already radioed for the authorities, yet my mother continued on this path of destruction.

The officer on the scene arrested my mother for shoplifting, otherwise known as stealing. Irrespective of her mental capacity, she was a thief and had taken "another person's property without permission or legal right." I still remember the spacey look on my mother's face as they placed her in handcuffs and in the backseat of the officer's car. And even still, I remember the compassion of the officer that escorted me to the backseat of his vehicle, no handcuffs, but a heart heavily burdened by the misguided actions of my mother. The officer spoke in kind, gentle words through the wired partition separating us. He asked about my family and explained to me what would happen to my mother. Unaware of her mental illness, he'd informed me that she'd go to jail, as that is the law for individuals that steal.

Twenty-two years later, I'd found myself connected to yet another mentally disturbed person, and as a result of their warped way of thinking, I'd once again straddled the back seat of a police car, been transported to this unknown, and was now staring down the many shades of uncertainty. Only this time, there was no comforting conversation through a wired partition … no hopeful reassurances. There was just the blaring silence that was now roaring in this bedroom where I sat alone. Sitting in my quiet room, glaring at those damn white socks, I realized that someone had stolen from me! This time, the cunning assailant hadn't stolen some cheap body spray or fashion jewelry. He'd called into question my sanity and in doing so, had taken every shred of freedom I'd once enjoyed. My days would now be spent under a watchful eye, with timed showers and a one-on-one session for me to shave my armpits. There was *no choosing* not to be hungry, as mealtime was as orchestrated as group therapy. There was *no choosing* when to get some fresh air, as one hour per day was allotted to being outside, white socks and all. There was *no choosing* the view, as there was but one view from the small window in my room—that of a fenced-in area with a bench that no one ever sat on. There was *no choosing* what outfit to rock for the day or which coordinating shoes to don, as the only *outfit* I had was the maxi dress I'd arrived in and the white socks the hospital had provided. There was *no choosing* … no freedom.

My husband was a thief, to say the least, yet he hadn't been cuffed, read his rights, or hauled off to some holding cell. He was resting comfortably at the home I'd made and with sons I'd struggled to birth. This man had stolen from me, and it wasn't the penny candy my grandmother had cautioned us to not touch in the supermarket. My husband had not only stolen my freedom but more importantly, my reality! He'd stolen my thoughts and actions, manipulated them, and regurgitated false truths. If I'd questioned his mother's random showing up at our house on a chaotic Monday night for dinner, my husband would calmly tell me, "Remember I told you she was coming over for dinner tonight instead of Friday... oh, but you're so busy with the kids, you probably just got the days mixed up." I'd stand in the kitchen for minutes on end recanting the conversation in my head, certain that we'd agreed upon Friday night, not Monday. Then, there would be the times when my husband would just up and leave to hang out with his co-residents. On his way out the door, I'd ask my husband where he was going or what was going on. Again, he'd nicely state, "Oh, I told you we had a resident retreat going on tonight and that I had to be there... but you were probably doing something with the boys when I told you and you don't remember." And finally there were the mornings I'd wake up extra early to fit in a workout before getting our sons ready for school and my heading off to work. I'd awaken at 5:30 a.m. to find that my doting husband had already left for a clinic that didn't open until 8:30 a.m. When confronted with the facts, my husband would offer his favorite response, "You must be overwhelmed. I told you I had to go in early today." I'd even begun to write everything down, yet I couldn't stop the robbery in progress. Now, I sat in this asylum, imprisoned for the actions of my assailant.

A thief assumes ownership of those things that don't belong to him. To my husband, I was his property—mind, body, and soul. By choosing myself over him and demanding a divorce, I'd pissed off my thief. I'd interrupted his robbery, disrupted his plan. This was the ultimate threat to everything he knew. I'd later come to learn "aggressive personalities are always looking for an excuse to go to war. So, they will construe any sort of hostility as an 'attack' and feel justified in launching an offensive".[8] *Stealing* was my husband's lifestyle, and the thought of the compromise and embarrassment that comes with divorce was too much to handle. My leaving him—the prominent, good doctor that he'd touted himself to be—was so far removed from winning that I simply had to go. The idea of my husband surrendering to anyone equaled defeat and total arrest. This narcissist simply wasn't having it. My husband's depraved indifference for my life was evident as was the truth about who he really was. My husband no longer was. He was nothing more than a common thief.

Over the course of my infelicitous stay, I'd poured out love to strangers, and in turn, had received more love in 96 hours than I'd ever experienced in seven years of loving someone I thought I knew. I'd found that in this place called Greenleaf, irrespective of the different means by which we'd gotten there, we were all the same ... individuals fighting for or against something. Some were battling depression, thoughts of self-harm, skeletons of the past, anger, lies. Nonetheless, we were fighting. I recalled with my newfound friends the series of painful and shocking events that had led to my being in Greenleaf. For the first time ever, I bore my soul about the abuse I'd suffered at the hands and mouth of my husband. And I openly expressed my fears of what was yet to come. But thanks to these remarkable human beings, I was prepared to weather the storm ahead.

Welcome Home

It's been said "Home is where the heart is." *So, where do I call home now that my heart has been broken?* was the question, I asked myself as I walked out of the doors to freedom. Tuesday, August 20, 2013, I processed out of Greenleaf to return home to my psychopath. The love I'd discovered in Greenleaf was now displaced. The feelings that I felt at that very moment led me to recall a conversation I'd had with one of the women at Greenleaf. Here, I shall call her Joan. I'd made it no secret that my first mission upon discharge was to divorce my nemesis. Joan had shared with me her experience with divorce. She'd paralleled her divorce to the grief one experiences with death. She'd talked about the initial shock that comes with the realization that the marriage is actually over, followed by the roller coaster of emotions thereafter. Now, in her second marriage, Joan readily identified what was happening. She was cascading through the stages of grief, a reality that had *voluntarily* brought her to Greenleaf.

On the drive home, Joan's words moshed around in my head along with thoughts of the real world I'd soon be faced with. One thing for certain was that I was grieving. In no uncertain terms, I was dancing in the anger stage of grief .[9] I'd had five days in my maxi dress and white socks to dance with denial. Now, I was angry, furious, mad as hell. With the certainty of divorce, there were oh so many uncertainties. How were my children? What lies had been told to them in

69

my absence? Did and would they understand that Mommy didn't just up and leave them but had been coerced to by the most monumental act of malicious force, hatred, and betrayal? What about my job, and how would my career be impacted by this? What would people think, and how would I deal with all the unspoken words that silence a small community? The more I thought over these things, the more pissed I'd become.

As we pulled into the long driveway, my soul shuttered. A place that I'd once called home was foreign to me. I felt like I'd forgotten how to open the car door and, even more so, walk. I commanded my body to go through the motions. I opened the side door to walk into the house. There was no fanfare, just the sting of my narcissist sitting at the peninsula reading the paper. He looked up at me and candidly said, "Welcome home." The profundity of his depravity was incomprehensible. I glared at him as I commenced to walk through the house to find my two little boys that were not there. My brother, who had driven me, had stepped back outside to engage in conversation with my husband. I didn't even bother to say goodbye to my brother... I closed myself off in the owner's suite and slipped into a hot bath, hoping to wash away this nightmare.

Moments later, the joys of my life ran in! I burst into tears and snatched them up, one by one, into the tub with me, clothes, shoes, and all. I smelled them, rubbed their chubby cheeks, and held them so close. I cried as I told them how much I loved them and how I'd missed them. There were no words to express the joy racing through my soul. My heart was broken, but my soul leaped for these two beautiful little boys. I'd had two painful miscarriages prior to the birth of my now three-year-old son. This moment felt closest to the joy I'd felt on seeing his little round face emerge at birth. Uninterrupted, my sons played in the water as I marveled over them. This joy would last for but a moment, for I knew of the journey that awaited me.

The next day, Wednesday, August 21, 2013, I returned to work, an act that used to be so routine, so natural, so effortless, and would now prove to be a day-to-day battle with my newly crafted demons. There were the whispers, the looks, and my favorite (seriously, no sarcasm) the straightforward question: *What happened?* I'd spend most of my nine-hour shifts in the bathroom, throwing up, crying, or both at the same time. This new actuality was too much, too painful, so unimaginable, so unreal yet all the while very real. After a few days of doing this, I smartened up and threw some Visine° eye drops into my all-essential makeup bag. Once the tears had subsided, I'd drop a couple of drops into each eye, reapply mascara, and return to the pharmacy counter as though nothing had happened. And then there were my glasses, another essential tool in my evolving coping-mechanisms box. Each of my "live births" had given me the gift of a son, stretch marks, and a little something extra. With the birth of my oldest son, this extra something was high blood pressure. And with my youngest son, there was the gift of vision changes. In this critical time in my life, I was thankful for the latter gift and thankful to wear glasses. I quickly discovered that the brighter the frame, the more distracting. It was difficult for my patients and coworkers to see the pain, the fatigue, the stress in my eyes when these elements were concealed behind flashy frames. So I had prescription lenses installed in nothing less than vibrant, colorful frames—yellow ones, blue ones, purple ones, and my favorite pair, the Guess° acetate red frames. These red frames quickly became my go-to look as people would look at my face, yet not *see* me—not see the pain, the fatigue, the stress. People would only *see* what it was I needed them to see, these super flashy red glasses and my brick red lips to match.

The Arena

Something as painful as wrongful commitment is debilitating. The landscape of life is tarnished, never again to be the same. The road to reckoning and recovery is cobblestoned, demarcated by these little shitty pebbles that seem to stick to the bottom of your shoe, giving way to this never ending stench. My journey to peace has taught me that this road is messy and certainly is not meant to be traversed alone. I have found that God gives each of us our own individual paths to take. No matter how many times we're thrown off course or voluntarily detour, our ordained course remains. In the midst of such a shitty situation, the beauty lies in having the courage to reach out to those closest to you and trusting those individuals to travel the shitty cobblestoned path with you.

Three of my closest cousins braved the shit storm with me. They waltzed right into the poo pond and sang the old spiritual, Kumbaya, as I sought for understanding, healing, and the rite of passage to move forward. Only years older than me, these women, my cousins, bear the wisdom of ages. Products of Tenth Street, each of us share similar life stories, rich with successes and equal failures. The eldest, Shannon, boasts a doctorate in education; Tabitha, a master's degree in counseling; and Tyneisha, a degree in environmental engineering. As the youngest of Dolan's granddaughters, I'd always admired my cousins, their beauty, and their skill sets.

Over the years, I'd grown to lean into them for support, clarity, and guidance. At this juncture in my life, however, I did more than just lean in. At the feet of the one that always assumes this naturally mothering role to each of us, me and her sisters alike, I collapsed. I was lost, broken, defeated by lies, pinned down by pain. Tabitha became my surrogate, my counselor, my prayer warrior, my voice.

Somehow, Tabitha managed to balance that fine line of "telling you like it is" with care and compassion. She was sure to tell me that the road ahead would be bumpy at best, but that I am a Hudson and I could do it! Tabitha reminded me that I'd survived the hell of growing up in the sheer definition of dysfunction and that my husband's antics were but a mere comedy in comparison. Her words spoke strength to my brokenness and healing to my wounds. On one occasion, I recall a telephone conversation with Tabitha. I was more than 250 miles away from anything remotely close to home. With my face planted in some nasty carpet, I sobbed into the phone, metaphorical white flag of surrender in the air. And then, Tabitha took me ringside to one of the greatest fights of all times.

She described to me the gruesome scene as two boxers go round for round in the boxing ring. Punches are thrown, jabs land. The opponent is left worn, bruised, and oftentimes bloodied. Nevertheless, the two fight on. The battle ensues until the bell sounds. Tabitha went on to depict that moment when the boxers go into their respective corners for relief, attention, and advice from the team of coaches and staff that await them. In the corner, petroleum jelly is applied to the face to help each punch slide off; butterfly bandages are applied to the broken skin; and, the boxer is given some sort of fluid to rehydrate. When the bell sounds again, Tabitha continued, the boxers get back up, pound their fists together, and march back to center ring to fight. "So even though you're down right now, all bruised up in your corner, you have to get up and fight!" Tabitha said. Her words resonated through my soul! My cry dissipated to a sniffle. It was high time for me to fight!

It's funny when a newcomer steps into the ring with a life veteran boxer. He thinks his antics and clever ruse will surmount in victory. The novice dances around the ring, landing a jab here and there. He may even find that his crafty moves land the champ face down on the mat. What the challenger fails to realize, however, is that the veteran is seasoned in the art of fighting, and though he has been face down many times before, his victory lies in what happens when he gets back up. While the rookie glares down at his opponent, jeering defeat, the veteran quietly chuckles as this prostrate position represents a time of redemption. Time to rest, if only but for a moment, to carefully strategize, and prepare to begin again. History has taught this experienced fighter how to silence the roar of the crowd, dissect the fight style of his opponent, and adapt his own skill to conquer the enemy. For the master, this is but another fight, and as he has delivered in the past, his victory is imminent!

Thus is how I viewed the nebulous plot of my husband. He'd schemed, plotted, lied to have me wrongfully committed. An insidious act that had definitely knocked me down. There I lay in the arena, face down in pain, bloody with shame, bruised by defeat. There I lay, for what seemed like an eternity. I'd been in the ring since the age of three, fighting the singe of my mother and father's divorce, overcoming the gift of two impossible parents, and rebuking the curse of times forecasted upon my life. In the present fight, I stammered to even come to one knee. I could hear the commentators, their treacherous whispers as salt to my wounds. The bell rang. I crawled into my corner, tears pouring from my swollen eyes. While Tabitha and my other prayer warriors were busy tending to the wreckage, my muscle memory awakened. I'd been down before but not like this. This was brutally painful. I didn't know if I could survive another round. But I knew I had to fight! For my very life and the lives of the two little boys I loved most, I had to fight!

Emancipation

My husband had stolen so much from me that I really had little left to lose. There was still, however, epic loss. In a matter of days, I'd dropped weight that compared only to persons stricken with a debilitating illness, in excess of twelve pounds per week and counting. I simply couldn't eat. I'd prepare hot breakfast and dinner for my sons, and not even do a taste test. I was stressed out beyond comprehension, beyond any breath of words. I lay clinched in the grips of agony, so eating had to wait its turn. Along with the physical loss went my hair. I'd always prided myself in having this thick, kinky beautiful hair. Even this hair, however, was not built to withstand the deceit, lies, betrayal, and pain of the days it now endured. Overnight, my entire crown went bald. Not thinned out … bald. The stress, added dietary deficiencies, and sleep deprivation were too much on my body and definitely too much on my hair. I'd resolved to wear extensions to conceal the loss, all in hopes of holding on to some outward manifestation of the woman I'd once known. And then there was my home. The outward, physical manifestation of my hard work … a true testament to the fruit of labor. My home had once represented the cavity of my spirit, this being I'd molded into love. Over time, however, this place had morphed into my prison, so I freely walked away. I was granted one weekend to pack up my "personal affects." Little did I know that "personal affects" would not confer to my sons.

My husband and his family were rooted in this town so they knew people, they knew the system, and they knew how to move and operate in this system. This was a game of chess, and I'd grown up knowing only how to play spades. With my husband on my cellphone plan, I was able to go back and ascertain when he'd first made contact with his attorney. I was shocked to learn that while I was yet pleading for a divorce, fighting out this marriage, he'd already been in contact with his attorney and was getting his game plan together. My husband had always been quite the perfectionist, and this would be no different. He'd orchestrated the perfect plan and had patiently awaited this judge's turn at seat. On the morning of October 8, 2013, I'd opened the garage door to find the county sheriff waiting outside. My oldest son asked, "Mommy, why is the policeman here?" as the officer served me with divorce papers that had been drawn up more than a month prior. The chief judge was up for rotation and would preside over my case.

I wasn't from this town, but when asked by the locals who was presiding over my case, each time my answer was met with this more than unsettling response. This judge's reputation preceded him by every stretch of the imagination. Fresh out of law school, he'd been arrested for driving under the influence of marijuana and his run-ins with the very legal system he was sworn to uphold had not yet come to an end. In 2005, he'd been arrested and charged with assault (one count of battery and two counts of simple battery) for an attack against his then girlfriend. Six years later, this chief judge was charged, yet again, with driving under the influence (of alcohol) with an open container in the vehicle.

Most interestingly, however, was this judge's own personal separation. This judge had reportedly gone through a very nasty, public divorce that had since left him irrationally disfigured. The locals described him as having this "hatred for women" and as being one that was "quick to give the kids to the dad." Not a single person spoke to the contrary, and countless people spoke. Each depiction was dreadfully the same story, just shared by a different party.

Naturally, I shared my concerns with my lawyer. Even though I didn't know this judge and I didn't have any evidence of his alleged private affairs, I was concerned. I could not help but think my fate had already been decided long before I'd ever entered his courtroom. My lawyer had made it really clear to me that this was the "chief judge" and there was "no getting reassigned." This was it. My husband had once braggingly told me, "The shield is real," not in the *biblical* sense of the word 'shield' but in the *all about who you know* definition of the word. This was home field advantage, and I would now appreciate the life behind his words. I was on his turf, isolated in his safe zone. I had no strategy aside from truth and no perfectly well thought out, calculated plan. I'd not been at this thing since day one, yet sat here at ground zero trying to pick up the pieces.

Chapter 5 of Title 19 of the Official Code of Georgia Annotated provides thirteen statutory grounds for divorce.[10] While most of us think about things like adultery and cruel treatment, there is one statute I'd never even heard of— incurable mental illness. Indeed, my husband had done his homework in setting the tone for my destruction. This was, by all means, a concerted attack against my character, against my life, against my mind. To say that "she's crazy" is one thing, but to escalate that salacious accusation to "she's been involuntarily institutionalized" for an incurable (only treatable) mental illness is an entirely different ballgame. Such is to accuse me of being unstable and to call into question my parenting capabilities. Such is to crush my spirit. Such is to destroy me and take away the two most precious lives I knew.

For over a year, I fought for my sons. In and out of court, exorbitant attorney fees, I fought! No one ever told me that part of my emancipation from my prison and its warden would mean losing my sons. Yet, on October 2, 2014, there I was ... seated in the chief judge's courtroom, hearing the cold words of swift injustice handed down. "I can't see two little black boys growing up in Augusta without their dad." There was silence as the Universe paused, as I sat encapsulated in the breath of the moment. I was frozen in time, frozen in this moment of time. I could hear my heart racing. I felt the leather of the chair beneath me shifting. Tears ran to the forefront of my face, having no respect for any boundaries. My red glasses clouded with wet fog. In this moment, there was no rationale, no logic, no law— not even a whiff of this judge calling into question my sanity. There was just this judge, the chief judge, and this immense injustice. There was blissful ignorance that reeked of bias and blatant partiality. "I can't see two little black boys growing up in Augusta without their dad." This was the chief judge. He had made his decision purely *because he could* and with the stinging flare of *I just did*. With fourteen words, this had become my new reality, a reality even more painful and stunning than its past. With these fourteen words, I had lost and had become not more than a mere surrogate to my "two little black boys."

This precipitous fight had rankled my psyche. It had come without warning. I'd had no time to train for battle. No morning workouts, no deep breathing techniques, not even a prayer. With a moment's notice, I was thrown into the ring. The private plane I'd been coasting on—this so-called wonderful thing called life—had been hijacked. Summer 2015, I looked to what Dr. Robin Stern calls my "flight attendant" for clarity, understanding, and guidance.[11] That flight attendant became more like my personal pilot. She'd become the equivalent of God's speaker box to the pain in my life. As a believer, I believe God works through the intangible *and* tangible to heal brokenness. There had to be something or someone in this world to assuage the pain. Not some recreational force or warm body to cuddle up to. Not a quick fix or numbing power. Tabitha's words reverberated with authority, "You have to heal and you need help to do that." I was now in search of that healing. A force certified to repair the schism that now served as a stronghold over my life.

I was sitting in a movie theatre watching "The Minions" with my sons when I realized that behind the 3-D glasses I was crying. This was my "assigned time" with the two most important people in my life.

I would like for you to close your eyes and imagine, for a moment, your life completely derailed by a lie. A lie that has now left you detached from the people you love most. If you are a parent, naturally, this agape love is unlike any other love than that which you have for your children. Imagine all the many times you'd feared the worst happening while pregnant with them. Imagine the joy of every prenatal visit, especially that overwhelmingly intense feeling when you first heard *that* heart beat. Imagine.

Imagine the exhilaration of labor day—the moment you welcomed the love of your life, your flesh, into the world. "Happy Birthday," you whispered to your sleeping angel. Imagine every night spent rocking the love of your life to sleep, all the while losing sleep as you stare at the monitor or tip toe into the nursery, so sleep deprived that you can hardly see the ever present rise and fall of your little one's chest as each soft breath is taken. Imagine the thrill of the crawl. Imagine cheering on his or her first step. Imagine each of these precious moments shared with your child on your own volition… precious moments … time not allocated, not intermittently apportioned but experienced freely.

Now imagine this time undermined by the grossly unfair repercussions of a premeditated, intentional lie. Imagine all the *firsts* you've missed out on because *that first* didn't occur on a first, third, or alternating fifth weekend. Imagine your lifetime of nighttime check-ins limited to the gravity of forty-eight hours. Imagine having to pin down every moment and every vacation well in advance, as every minute holds the breath of your new life of memories. Imagine.

For me, this "assigned time" with my sons was precious, invaluable. It was, however, our time, and my goal was always to make the best of it. There was no time for anger, no time for sadness, no time for grieving. But here I was—crying. In the midst of this comic-filled adventure, my subconscious had been busy retracing and reevaluating my entire life. My psyche was in turmoil ... every part of me in undeniable pain. It was time to find the *help* Tabitha had been speaking of. At this finite moment in my life, it was interesting to take notice that even with my mother's battles with mental illness, there was never talk about counseling, therapists, the like. Growing up on Tenth Street, God was the immediate source of all healing. In my universe, I'd often envision Him making this physical, yet supernatural, descent to earth each time there was one of us in need of some sort of healing. Seriously, there was just this overwhelmingly silent stigma against such talk of therapists. It was almost as though it were blasphemy to even mention the word *therapist*. You were definitely labeled "crazy" with even a leaked thought along these lines. For every tribulation, there was God and God alone, and I'd been raised to seek Him out as the ultimate counselor. I, however, had grown beyond the confounds of my upbringings and was now centered in my own beliefs so much so as to respect that sometimes God communicates with us through other people. And sometimes these people aren't our pastor, aren't friends, aren't family...

but therapists, counselors, psychiatrists. There would be this leap of faith in the line of actions that followed this path of growth, beliefs, and thinking.

There I sat in this movie theatre … in darkness … this internal and external darkness. I eased my phone from my purse and typed "therapist augusta georgia" in the internet search field. A number of practices and providers popped up, so I know it must have been God that led me to this woman named Julie Keck. July 17, 2015, in the bathroom at a movie theatre, I made the single call that reshaped the topography of my life. That following Monday, July 20, 2015, a little before 9:00 a.m., I found myself seated in the small waiting area of Resolution Counseling Professionals. A million thoughts raced through my brain as I looked around at the antique finished, white distressed furniture. I wasn't sure whether to cross or uncross my legs… sit with my back erect or relaxed. I looked down at my turquoise colored, worn Brooks', questioning if I should have dressed more business casual as opposed to the black yoga pants I'd chosen to throw on. *Is my oversized t-shirt okay?*, I thought. Would I need to take my shoes off as I stretched out on this emerald green couch or….? As my nervous thoughts trailed on, this tall blonde appeared from the white door. She spoke my first name and introduced herself as Julie. I nervously shook her hand and followed her down this short hallway that led to her office.

The office was a softly decorated 12 by 10 foot space. I couldn't help but wonder if this space was big enough to accommodate the guilt and shame that I had just brought into it. In contrast to the emerald green couch I'd imagined, there was an earth-toned couch positioned against the longer wall with an accent table to its right. At its left was a large window with the sunlight casting beautifully off the pastel-colored paint. The wall was lined with a bookcase and a sofa chair stationed before it. I'd never been in formal counseling before, so I wasn't sure if I was supposed to lie on the couch or sit. I chose to simply sit. I sat across from Julie as this shell of the woman I'd used to be. I wasn't sure how or where to begin, so I opened our session with those words, something to the effect of "I don't know where to start." I took off my red glasses and sat there, transparent, ashamed, and heavy laden. I very openly spoke of the source of my pain, my husband. I shared with Julie my involuntary institutionalization at Greenleaf, and I shared with her the grief of now having lost my sons. It was like word vomit, with no tears, no big words, no lies, no secrets. Yes, though a stranger by all means, this woman was now my therapist, and if there was any hope, any inkling of a chance in her helping me, I had to have her know everything, in truth and honesty. As I spoke to her, I felt face down in the arena, again. There I was, in those white socks, walking the halls of Greenleaf as I recalled all that had led to this very moment. It was as though I'd reopened each bandage for Julie to inspect the scars, just to find the sutures torn and blood weeping from them. It hurt. I hurt.

After I was done giving Julie the Cliffs Notes version of my personal hell, I expressed to her the following, "I want you to help me." I explained to her what I'd envisioned this *help* to look like. I'd been in practice as a pharmacist for nine years and was well aware of the importance of medication in various clinical settings. I didn't profess to be this know-it-all or this person void of acceptance. What I was, however, was someone who understood that prescription medications are sometimes essential elements in the overall treatment plan. These plans, however, are individualized. And just how one person's high blood pressure can be managed with diet and exercise alone, and the next individual might require a litany of medications, I went into therapy with this clear perception of *my* goals and *my* capacity. This was *my* life, *my* trauma, *my* experience, *my* story. And until proven otherwise, I would continue on this drug free path of managing *my* mental health. I explained to Julie that I didn't want medications… I didn't want to mask, conceal, or diminish the hurt that I'd experienced… I didn't want to ignore the pain. I wanted to face it—this unimaginable pain—and in facing it, I wanted to learn how to make it go away. Nonetheless, as my therapist, I would respect Julie's professional opinion and recommendations, even if she'd believed medication to be an integral part of *my* plan. My sixty minutes were almost up as Julie and I agreed to the task at hand. I'd committed to therapy every week, even multiple times a week if that's what it would take. And I'd committed to the hard work, the journey of healing.

For every week, there was a therapy session. With every session, there was an assignment. With every assignment, there was purpose and there was healing. One thing for sure was this process would not be easy. I would not waltz into my therapist's office one day and miraculously be "healed." There was no sprinkling of holy water to rid my spirit and emotional self of all the hell I'd been through. There was no short cut, no "control+alt+delete" functionality that could rapidly reboot and reset this system. This was a process that entailed me processing the pain and trauma that had landed me in this very place. Process is defined as "a series of actions or steps taken in order to achieve a particular end".[12] Every week in therapy I dedicated my inner being to the hard and painful work of processing and reckoning. Within the first three weeks of therapy, I'd come to understand that fear **is** a powerful thing! I'd allowed fear to bind me and, in turn, felt solely responsible for the current state in which I'd found my life. I'd blamed myself and punished myself by freezing time in this perpetual "time out." As a mom, I could appreciate the purpose of time outs. Only in this case, there was no two minutes in the corner to reflect, and then back to life at hand. There was daily reprimand and self-castigation. I'd conquered the first two steps of this process—making that all important phone call and walking into my first session—so now I would press forward in this involuted sequence ... this process of healing. The next stop would land me at the front door of forgiveness, forgiving myself for having stayed in such an unhealthy, abusive, toxic relationship. Through this door lies my breakthrough, as now a slightly more refined version of myself was better suited to navigate the full paradigm of what this "toxic" nature really meant.

Gaslighting

A pivotal moment in my recovery process occurred when Julie imparted insight into what I'd been describing as control, manipulation, and brainwashing from my spouse. She termed what happened (and had been happening) to me as gaslighting. Such a foreign term created an overwhelming sense of fear and release, all at the same time. I'd been gaslighted! It sounded like a newly discovered disease. I had no idea what gaslighting meant, but what I did know was this—I'm not crazy! As a person with a background in science, there was this innate need to have a name assigned to things. Now, there was an assignment, yet I had no idea what it meant. Flooding with emotions, I struggled with tears and listened as my therapist continued. She explained gaslighting as this very calculated, systematic approach to emotional and psychological breakdown. She paralleled gaslighting to an "extreme form of brainwashing," designed to make one question their judgment, recall, and ultimately, their sanity. Julie continued by explaining this tactic as one commonly used by narcissists but, unfortunately, not often recognized by the intended party until it's too late. In my world, this translated into a psychological ambush.

To help my understanding of this form of abuse, Julie encouraged me to read this book called *In Sheep's Clothing*. As Julie spoke the words, *In Sheep's Clothing*, it was as though her lips moved in slow motion as my mind shuddered … *Innnnnnn*

Sheep'sssssss Clothingggggg. Years of Sunday school and Bible study had led me to reflect upon the scripture that speaks of just that. Matthew 7:15 warns "Watch out for false prophets. They come to you in sheep's clothing, but inwardly they are ferocious wolves." Verse 16 continues, "By their fruit, you will recognize them."

Two days later, the book arrived in the mail, and I continued on the journey to understanding this thing called gaslighting and the predator that had nearly destroyed my life. As the title implies, *In Sheep's Clothing* delves into the many personalities and characters we often encounter daily; some are disguised while others are pretty transparent. Author of this international bestseller, George Simon Jr., Ph.D., characterizes manipulative personalities and exposes many of the tools these persons underhandedly employ to best suit their own agenda and best achieve their personal goals. Simon details one's personality as "the distinctive interactive "style" or relatively ingrained way a person prefers to deal with a wide variety of situations and to get the things they want in life".[13]

One of the personalities described in the opening content of this book was home to the person I'd married and had children with, and to whom the rolling credits could thank for my *almost* having lost it all. This is the covert-aggressive personality. Simon introduces this character by laying out scenarios in which the victims disregard that small voice that screams something is wrong. With each case, Simon explains the victim "felt on the defensive, but consciously they had trouble seeing their manipulator as merely a person on the offensive … they ended up feeling crazy".[14] The reality was these people, like me, were fighting! And this wasn't some *overt* battle that could readily be identified, analyzed, and more appropriately responded to. The people in these scenarios and me were engaged in a losing battle with the *covert* entity alluded to in scriptures, such as Ephesians 6:12: "For our struggle is not against flesh and blood, but against the rulers, against the authorities, against the powers of this dark world and against the spiritual forces of evil..." According to Simon, "manipulative people are expert at fighting in subtle and almost undetectable ways ... you don't even know you're in a fight until you're well on your way to losing".[15] This covert-aggressive personality "can be ever so ruthless in their interpersonal conduct while concealing their aggressive character or perhaps even projecting a convincing, superficial charm".[16]

As I read *In Sheep's Clothing*, it became clearer to me that while I'd survived the most evident adversaries of my time, life had not yet prepared me for the one contender that would silently try to destroy me. "Covert-aggressives are ruthlessly ambitious people but they're careful not to be perceived that way".[17] At the heart of the covert-aggressive personality is this sheer drive to win, a motivation that spares no expense. This personality "can be deceptively civil, charming, and seductive"[18] and equally "adept at fighting unscrupulously yet surreptitiously".[19] For my husband, for the covert-aggressive personality, there was no glory in conceding, no glory in divorce, no glory in being made to look bad, no glory in perceived loss. His victory lay in wait with my defeat.

Covert-aggressives "know how to 'look good' and how to win you over by 'melting' your resistance".[20] There was one occasion during our courtship when my husband, then "guy in the blue scrubs," had presented me with a book about pugs. In previous conversation, I'd expressed to him how much I loved pugs. I was eating lunch with a group of girlfriends in the hospital cafeteria when he came up to me and handed me this book. He went on to say that "even though I can't buy you a pug right now, I thought you should have this." He was such the sharp dresser and an ever so smooth talker with the gift of gab.

But in the present moment, the actuality of divorce was more than a wrinkle in his perfect little outfit. "Covert-aggressive personalities are adept at charming, praising, flattering, or overtly supporting others in order to get them to lower their defenses and surrender their trust and loyalty".[21] Great at sporting this duplicity of character, my husband vocally put forth that I "had to be crazy" as to not want to continue to live under the thumb of such covert aggression.

The disturbed covert-aggressive personality willfully deploys a number of tactics to manipulate his victims, including lying, denial, rationalization, diversion, shaming, and guilt-tripping. While I'd lived through all of these, I'd found most astonishing the power of a lie, as my husband had repeatedly lied to others in telling them that I'd "wanted to kill myself," an ominous act that had landed me in Greenleaf. His lies were so pervasive. When I'd refused to be silent about what he'd done, there was his vehement denial, defined as "when the aggressor refuses to admit that they've done something harmful or hurtful when they clearly have".[22] Then, there was so much shaming. This is when the covert-aggressor uses "subtle sarcasm and put-downs as a means of increasing fear and self-doubt".[23] Spend just one minute, let alone five days, involuntarily confined in a psychiatric facility and mental health becomes quite the sensitive subject. While I'd fostered an appreciation for those that battle the relentless grip of mental health, I'd developed an equally pure disdain for my husband's hurtful, insensitive shaming tactics. There were the piercing glances, curt responses, and there were always the covert threats of never seeing my sons again. When this fear mongering wasn't brutal enough in crushing my spirit, there was the rhetorical aggrandized shaming, like "Are you on your medication?" "Have you taken your meds today?" or flat out, "You're crazy!" oftentimes hurled in front of my children.

"One of the more sinister ways the most manipulative covert-aggressors (i.e., psychopaths) disadvantage their victims [is by] gaslighting".[24] The history of the word gaslighting comes from the 1938 stage play and adapted 1944 American film *Gaslight*, wherein the husband tries to slowly manipulate his wife into thinking she's going crazy. The husband goes to great lengths to isolate his wife then commences to strategically move things around the house as to create this sense of doubt in the wife. In one instance, the husband removes an heirloom brooch that the wife had stored away in her purse. When she discovers it missing, the husband asserts that the wife, herself, had moved it. The controlling, manipulative husband continues to change and move things around the house, including dimming the flame on a gas light, as to convince the wife that she is indeed going crazy.

I was miserable in my marriage, even depressed as my covert-aggressor was so good at pulling the wool over my eyes that I didn't realize I'd been under attack until it was too late. From day one, this man had manipulated my every thought, move, action, until I'd found myself at this place in time, alone and under siege. First rule of the hunt is to separate the prey from its pack. My husband had carefully declined residency offers as to ensure his place back *home*. I'd argued for a more neutral location, but had failed to appreciate the strength of the covert-aggressor when operating in familiar territory. With me isolated and him on his own turf, this voracious apex predator definitely had the upper hand. What's interesting about an apex predator that sets him apart from all other predators, is that there is no other animal in their habitat strong enough to hunt them. Immersed in his habitat, I stood not a chance. When I'd *asked* to go home to visit my family, there was always a reasonable explanation or a rationalization for why such a visit would be prohibitive. The same excuses were offered up when my family would ask to come visit me. Damn near every petition from me was met with a fierce "No" from him … with the occasional "Let me think about it," as though I were asking for parental consent. Even my trips to the gym or simple Target run were met with reproach, always seen as "not spending enough time at home." So long as I was taking care of and buying for his family, my husband saw me as "kind," "good-hearted," "caring," "a blessing to the family." Yet the minute I bought anything for my family, I was called "manic," "impulsive," "irrational," and "irresponsible." For eight years, I'd been gaslighted and not just by my husband but also by his family.

When the manipulator feels his tactic is working but not quite achieving optimal effect, other strategies are employed. The objective of the covert-aggressor is to win, and sometimes this entails the team approach. The covert-aggressor will engage in what Simon calls "a reality and history restructuring campaign, subtly coaching relatives and friends to remember things as happening the way they want them to be remembered and then pointing out to the person being gaslighted that they are the only person who remembers things differently".[25] This is a well-orchestrated, coordinated attack against the target of gaslighting. It involves an alliance between willing participants, precise timing in execution, and this artistry that's unmatched. I call this behavior synchronized gaslighting. The parties engaged in the mechanics of this behavior are accomplices to the same crime of psychological and emotional abuse.

My first attempts at reading this book were thwarted by sheer pain as I relived the agony and hurt dealt by my abuser. I'd experienced firsthand the toxic effects of the covert-aggressive personality, the wolf in sheep's clothing. In processing this truth, Julie suggested I read this book entitled *Daring Greatly*. I'd grown to trust Julie with the very essence of my life, so I ordered the book. Two days later, *Daring Greatly* arrived, and I quickly began to read. Little did I know I'd opened a book to words that would forever transform my life. The author of *Daring Greatly*, Brené Brown, is a qualitative researcher at the University of Houston Graduate College of Social Work. She has devoted years of research to what I call and appreciate as those T-N-T topics … *tough-n-touchy* topics. Issues like empathy, vulnerability, and that oh so heavy "s" word, shame.

Right there, within the first few hundred words of this book, was the thing that had given birth to my present state, this construct called vulnerability. I'd always thought of vulnerability by its more traditional definition, the definition that most of us would agree makes us grossly uncomfortable and totally sucks – "the quality or state of being exposed to the possibility of being attacked or harmed, either physically or emotionally".[26] Okay, honestly, the thought of exposure to harm, in any fashion, just doesn't sit well in my universe. Brené, however, brought a different perspective to the word's meaning. She introduces vulnerability by opening the narrative with this epic passage from Theodore Roosevelt's speech "Citizenship in a Republic," a speech that is sometimes referred to as "The Man in the Arena." I'd never even heard of this speech but was forced to close the book when I read Brown's epigraph, this blazing intro into what it truly means to dare greatly. In honor of my ignorance of this moving body of work, I share this passage from Roosevelt's "Citizenship in a Republic"[27] speech:

It is not the critic who counts; not the man who points out how the strong man stumbles, or where the doer of deeds could have done them better.

The credit belongs to the man who is actually in the arena, whose face is marred by dust and sweat and blood; who strives valiantly; who errs, who comes short again and again, because there is no effort without error and shortcoming; but who does actually strive to do the deeds; who knows great enthusiasms, the great devotions; who spends himself in a worthy cause; who at the best knows in the end the triumph of high achievement, and who at the worst, if he fails, at least fails while daring greatly, so that his place shall never be with those cold and timid souls who neither know victory nor defeat.

This passage speaks to the epitome of what it means to be brave, to have the courage to show up, the tenacity to be fearless in the wake of so much more. Brené asserts that "This is vulnerability …Vulnerability is not knowing victory or defeat, it's understanding the necessity of both; it's engaging. It's being all in".[28] "Vulnerability is not weakness" yet it is the willingness "to show up and let ourselves be seen" irrespective of the outcome.[29] Vulnerability is "uncertainty, risk, and emotional exposure".[30]

With my husband, I'd been vulnerable by every sense of the word. I'd shown up and allowed all of me to be seen, even the parts that weren't so pretty and damn sure weren't comfortable. This was my husband … my supposed life partner … my supposed best friend. I'd engaged with this man, laid out all of my vulnerabilities, told him everything about my mother, from every suicide attempt to every institutionalization. I'd shared with him the pain of each of these moments I'd lived, as but the child that I was. I'd told my husband how sometimes it was like my mother was a different person—hell, different persons—all together. Surely I'd engaged. I'd unquestionably been all in. I'd been transparent, and now I'd been betrayed by false intimacy. My cunning husband had taken the plight of my mother and had made it my own. He'd crafted her mental illness to now be my story. He'd created this new, fictitious narrative of my life and had not even given me a chance to look over the script. I'd been blindsided. I'd been gaslighted.

He'd said I was "crazy" … He'd proclaimed I was "bipolar" (and not in that insensitive joking context of the word). My husband had claimed that I wanted to kill myself. His words and his actions were calculated, premeditated. His intent was malicious. All of this was so very wrong, so brutally unfair. Unfair to me, unfair to my children, and unfair to the community of people that actually do brave mental illness. This was unfair and so unreal. Yet it was happening, not on accident but on purpose. And by all accounts, my husband had done this with purpose. My husband had admitted to having spent half the night before Greenleaf on the phone with his beloved sister, strategizing to "get me some help." He'd spoken at length with his sister, a graduate of Valdosta State University; someone undoubtedly familiar with the Valdosta area; someone now actively working in social services. Then, he'd spoken with his mother and also with his brother "to make arrangements." Yet all the while my husband was busy reaching out to his family—conspiring, ever so "concerned about my welfare," "worried" about my "rapidly declining mental capacity"—not once did he ever bother to call a single member of my family, not even my brother who holds a bachelors degree in counseling psychology and a masters in community psych. What a mangled web. In the face of his own deep-seated evil, my husband had chosen to use my past and my pain for his own glory. He'd chosen to lie. He'd chosen to make me and my mother the same person. He'd chosen this confabulation over truth.

"Sometimes a single confabulation can damage our sense of self-worth and our relationships".[31] I was two months away from my thirty-third birthday when Greenleaf happened. I'd lived and breathed my mother's condition for nearly thirty-three years, and my postgraduate studies had allowed me the opportunity to get even more acquainted with her daily struggles. I understood the physiology of her illness, and I also understood the family correlation and genetic propensities tied to her condition. Even in trying to help my mother and better grasp her daily life, I'd devoted a significant part of my residency training to working with the psychiatrists and medical staff to develop a mental health clinical rotation. At this juncture in my life, one thing for sure was that I was not my mother. I was not mentally ill. So to have someone— someone that claimed to have loved me, someone that had taken vows before the Universe to honor and respect me and to stand by my side as my husband, to have *that* person, whom I'd engaged with, whom I'd been more than vulnerable with—to have that person lie and betray me represented danger, harm, and the annihilation of vulnerability.

"Our willingness to own and engage with our vulnerability determines the depth of our courage and the clarity of our purpose; the level to which we protect ourselves from being vulnerable is a measure of our fear and disconnection".[32] Own. Courage. Clarity. Purpose. I held fast to these words as I wrestled with this thing called vulnerability. I'd devoted more than enough time to living in fear. It was time to move on. But in doing so, Julie and I would have to take on one of Brené's other T-N-T topics, shame. I'd sit in Julie's office and cry over just the simple thought of shame. This small little word caused me so much agony, weighted, unavoidable grief. "Shame is the intensely painful feeling or experience of believing that we are flawed and therefore unworthy of love and belonging".[33] It is recognized as "the master emotion"[34], and I stood stifled in its presence. With a single word, this solitary concept, Brené Brown had sized up the spirit of my brokenness. Shame, this "liar" and "story-stealer"[35], and here I was kneeling in its honor. "Shame derives its power from being unspeakable"[36], and so I'd kept silent. Buried deeply beneath the betrayal, pinned under the hurt, and suffocating betwixt lifetimes of pain was the looming shadow of shame. Just so much shame. The shame of my abuse; the shame of my stupidity; the shame of my losses; the shame of such a weighted injustice; the shame of rebuilding and starting over; the shame of my story.

Something powerful, darn near supernatural, happens when we own our story. "Shame derives its power from being unspeakable." So imagine what happens when we step out of the shadows of fear and snatch back that power we've given to something or someone else. "When we own our stories, we avoid being trapped as characters in stories someone else is telling"[37]. This means "reckoning with our feelings and rumbling with our dark emotions – our fear, anger, aggression, shame, and blame"[38]. With Julie, I learned to practice what Brené calls shame resilience. For me, this translated into the ability to say *This shit hurts and is really fucked up, but I'm okay.* (Okay, certainly not Brené's exact definition but the essence of shame resilience.)

Scripture is replete with accounts wherein a demonic force must first be named, identified, so that it may be exorcised. There was power in my now having a name for this emotional abuse termed *gaslighting,* and there would be freedom in its exorcism. My sessions with Julie were painful but awakened in me the spirit of my grandmother. Dollie was fierce, tenacious. This woman knew no fear, stared the enemy square in the face, and spoke victory over the impossible—all in the name of Jesus! With Julie, I uncovered this coded segment of my DNA. I'd been raised by this woman, and her intimate connection with me was now alive and not to be silenced. Dollie had seen my then husband for what he was while I stood beside him, eyes wide shut. It was now time for me to stand strong, in spite of the whispers, criticism, side-eyes, and different versions of my story that were being told. "Not speaking out is ordinary".[39] In wake of this extra-ordinary experience, it was high time for me to find my voice, to speak power to truth, to speak up about this abuse called gaslighting.

Beautiful Trauma

A s a kid, I'd played the piano and had since grown to love all facets of music. My undergraduate studies with the great Isaac Holmes had instilled in me the beauty of the artistry that girdles music. Thanks to the instruction and natural gifts of Professor Holmes, I'd grown a fondness for music that could hardly be explained by words. Along with journaling, working out, prayer, meditation, and hot baths, music had now become a part of what Julie refers to as my "toolbox," this ornate object that I could employ in times of stress, anxiety, sadness, extreme emotional discomfort.

There was this one particular day I found myself listening to the artist P!nk. I've always admired her strength as a woman and her societal independence as an artist. But this particular day, I just so happened to have looked down at the face of my phone. It wasn't the lyrics to the music that now had engulfed my attention but, instead, the title of the album jumped out at me. *Beautiful Trauma*.[40] I had an epiphany as I sat and listened. In this life, we're all guaranteed to have trauma. Doesn't matter if this trauma is in the form of a broken relationship, death of a loved one, or physical remnants of an accident. It is still trauma. The question then becomes "What do you do with that trauma?" "Of all the things trauma takes away from us, the worst is our willingness, or even our ability, to be vulnerable. There's a reclaiming that has to happen".[41]

The Universe has ordained trauma to be this ugly, grotesque shit none of us, if we're honest with ourselves, really wants to deal with. It's more comforting to tuck trauma into a corner for an incessant timeout. It's easier to pretend whatever *it* is never happened. It's quite difficult to even begin to fathom any beauty within trauma. But here it was, these words. *Beautiful Trauma.* This loaded phrase that forced me to have a powwow with my own self and figure out what to do with my own, not-even-pretty trauma.

"Our identities are always changing and growing, they're not meant to be pinned down. Our histories are never all good or all bad, and running from the past is the surest way to be defined by it. That's when it owns us. The key is bringing light to the darkness – developing awareness and understanding".[42] These words were so important to me and so pivotal in navigating my process. For me, the translation was simple: Our traumas (and victories) shape us, define our character, drive our ambitions. Was I to allow *this* trauma, added to all the preexisting traumas, to define me? Debilitate me? Brand me? Was life to simply come to a whirling stop because yet another person had hurt me, caused me unrelenting pain? Or was I willing to do what Julie calls "the hard work" necessary to regain or maybe, for the first time, gain control over my own destiny. This idea of owning my own destiny was so abstract to me… a foreign concept. Prior to this place in my life, I'd never really thought about what it meant to own my own destiny … be the person I wanted to be. I'd spent the last eight years of my life being someone else—the "doctor's wife," "her daughter-in-law." Julie had given me this amazing thing called permission—permission to feel, permission to breathe, and permission to safely part from all these pseudonyms and step into the fullness of my own self.

Group therapy opened the door to a concept I could envision, one that was far more attainable, darn near tangible. According to Brené Brown, "we feel most alive when we're connecting with others and being brave with our stories".[43] During my undergraduate studies at Paine College, I'd learned a plethora of poems, from Maya Angelou's "And Still I Rise" to "Mother to Son" by Langston Hughes. While pledging, however, I'd learned a poem that transformed the landscape of my life and spoke to the trauma that I'd now endured. My work with Julie and the strength harnessed in sharing my story with all these other brave women led me to recall this great literary piece written by William Ernest Henley entitled "Invictus".[44]

"Invictus" is Latin for unconquered. Each stanza of this Victorian poem speaks with so much power as written here:

> Out of the night that covers me,
> Black as the Pit from pole to pole,
> I thank whatever gods may be
> For my unconquerable soul.
>
> In the fell clutch of circumstance
> I have not winced nor cried aloud.
> Under the bludgeonings of chance
> My head is bloody, but unbowed.
>
> Beyond this place of wrath and tears
> Looms but the horror of the shade,
> And yet the menace of the years
> Finds, and shall find me, unafraid:

It matters not how strait the gate,
How charged with punishments the scroll,
I am the master of my fate:
I am the captain of my soul.

After one of my group sessions, I came home and placed handwritten and printed versions of this poem throughout my personal spaces. This masterful art, these powerful words of affirmation, reminded me that just as its author had overcome the adversity of amputation, I too would overcome the bloodshed of deeply cut lies and malicious concatenation that had led to my current horror of shade. Instead of just mere words on a page or verses etched in memory, "Invictus" took on this life form that could engage with me, sit with me, embolden me. Its message was simple. *This shit is messed up but you will be okay… this, too, shall pass.* However, it was up to me to regain control over my fate, realign with God's purpose for my life. There was the echo of a deeply-seated "I" statement. I had to stand firmly on the fact that "I am the master of my fate: I am the captain of my soul".[45]

Bound

There's this scene near the end of Marvel's blockbuster hit movie *Black Panther* where the Royal Talon Fighter is dispatched to take down cargo ships that are carrying specialized weapons.[46] If these cargo ships are not stopped, not intercepted, the weapons on board will reach their final destinations and their impact on the world detrimental on a scale that is unimaginable. Agent Ross, the pilot of the Royal Talon, understands the gravity of this situation and that the fate of the world depends on disrupting these aircrafts' mission. The cargo ships must be stopped, their ploy derailed.

Now the Royal Talon Fighter jet is this super bad ass, technologically advanced powerhouse aircraft designed, built, and used to transport the sovereign of Wakanda. The Royal Talon boasts the most sophisticated weaponry, can operate in stealth mode, and is nearly indestructible. Yet in this scene, while going after these rogue cargo ships, the Royal Talon Fighter finds itself bound, restrained by these strong electrical cables coming from two other cargo ships.[47] The cables are incredibly strong and their effects crippling. I've always been a huge movie buff, so what amazes me as I watch this scene is the equanimity of Agent Ross's character in the midst of this crisis. He doesn't come undone, toss his hands up in the air, and prepare to disembark the aircraft. Agent Ross does not disengage. He does not give up! Instead, Agent Ross calls out to the person that designed the Royal

Talon for help. Shuri commands Agent Ross, "Make an X with your arms".[48] In the next breath, she instructs him, "Now break it".[49] As Agent Ross commits these actions, a paramount force breaks the cables binding the Royal Talon. The Fighter aircraft is instantaneously released, set free. As I watched this scene, I could not help but parallel the symbolism to my own life.

I'd been gaslighted and the climax of this abuse, Greenleaf, had me bound. I was shackled to the pain, held in a death grip by so much loss. I donned my pain now much like a modern day scarlet letter. Nothing in my life was the same. I'd been reduced to seeing my sons every first, third, and alternating fifth weekend and then on the assigned holidays. I was bound by the cables of lies, the lies that were still ripe, and the lies that were still being told. I'd been destabilized, my core fractured, my spirit definitely held captive by a pain that it could not comprehend. I longed to be free, prayed for some sense of normalcy but knew not even where to begin. So I turned to my Designer. My grandmother used to tell me, "He causes his sun to rise on the evil and the good, and sends rain on the righteous and the unrighteous" (Matthew 5:45). When my inexperienced self would get all bent out of shape and couldn't understand the trials of life, Dolan would drop these nuggets of wisdom into my spirit, truths I could hold fast to. It was like when her joints would ache with bad weather silently approaching, she'd tell me, "Oh, it's gonna rain." She'd remind me that some things are absolute, guaranteed—none of us were exempt from the struggles of life. Dollie would explain that though we may feel undeserving of our situation, whatever the situation may be, we could rest assured that it would rain. It didn't matter if we were good or bad or if the situation was fair or unfair. God sent rain on the righteous and unrighteous. An indiscriminate rain. Right now, I was in a downpour. But my Designer had already equipped me with what I needed to break free.

Eradicating the poisonous effects of gaslighting is much like the skillful technique behind ridding your garden of weeds. Sometimes you can get down on your knees and pull up the nuisance, weed by weed. I call this approach prayer. Then there are times when you can use reinforcement in the form of weed killer to destroy the intruder. I call this collective or corporate prayer. But then, there's that moment you realize your efforts have been null and void because the weeds have so encroached upon your yard that their presence is nearly indestructible. This is when you call for backup! Not just a neighbor to lend gardening advice or a question bounced off the personnel at your local gardening store. This is when you call in the muscle—an individual or team of persons trained to take on the problem. Skilled in complete eradication of the culprit yet preservation of all that is good. This, I call intercession.

Julie provided this muscle, this trained, skilled intercession. She called out gaslighting by the toxic, corrosive abuse that it is, and coached me through the most difficult time of my life! With unmitigated strength and guidance, Julie taught me how to re-engage, re-center, re-focus, and re-move anything and any persons blocking me from my true destiny, including parts of self. This is a process, and the process damn sure ain't easy! It requires much work—work that entails dedication to therapy, even when the pain is overwhelming. Work that requires a willingness to share your story, even when you feel small, overshadowed by shame. Work that demands the trust to lean and depend on a higher authority to mend the brokenness. Work that graces you with the courage to forgive not just the other person, but yourself… over and over and over again. The hapless remnants of gaslighting can be debilitating. Nevertheless, this journey of emotional and spiritual rehabilitation has taught me that the work is never ending, yet a continuum on this path to true freedom and to redefining self, love, and relationships.

❧

Nothing Heavy. . . Just Coffee

I n the midst of my perfect storm, God sent me this equally imperfect being—yoked to meet me at my place of pain and brokenness, hand-crafted to travel life not ahead of me and not above me, but right alongside me. The rest of my ribs had been conceived years before my existence, had lived life in the shadows of hurt and disappointment, yet had remained unmoved, still choosing to be vulnerable, to be brave, to love again. I'd been robbed of my entire life—life as I knew it, life as I'd created it, life as I'd worked so hard for it to be. I'd been falsely accused of wanting to kill myself, yet here I was, too aware to give up and simply unwilling to die (man, such a bummer for my now ex-husband). And though, at times, the pain was so great that dying, in the purview of the meek would have offered more appeal, I was not that person. I wasn't sure why, but I was certain that I'd been called to carry this particular cross. My grandmother had always told me that God reserved his most challenging assignments for those whom He'd trusted most to carry them out. And though, at times (*hell, most of the time*) I'd prayed He'd trusted me a whole lot less and had passed this assignment on to the next (*I could promise Him I would not be upset, not in the least*), the reality was this was my assignment. And to surrender any more of my life, energy, time, emotional bank to the enemy was not part of the call. As I'd taken off my wedding band at Greenleaf, marking the absolute disconnect from my marriage, I'd solidified that moment in time with a speech. Yep, one of those angry, pissed-off-woman rants. And just as most women in these moments, I'd meant every last word. I'd assured my husband that I would move forward from this place of pain, that I would heal from his hurt, and that I would love again, spring forth life, again, cultivate life, again. As I spoke those words, I knew the reality of bringing those words to fruition would not be easy, but I also recognized that the same God that had led me to this assignment would see me through to its completion.

There are two kinds of pain in this world. Pain that hurts. Pain that alters.[50] I believe the two to be inseparable and that we are naturally altered by hurt, transformed by pain. Sometimes the pain is so big, so great, that we can't hide it. Better yet, we don't want to hide it. This is where I found myself when I met my Chapter 12. I was living in pain, a pain that hurt and was actively altering. Life after Greenleaf posed a number of challenges, one being keeping my bills paid and not losing everything to bankruptcy. My husband had abruptly stopped his direct deposit into our checking account, covertly funneling funds to a separate checking account at an entirely separate bank. Fate would have it that I'd discovered his bank slip hidden in a dresser chest drawer while packing up my things—a secret account boasting in excess of twenty-four thousand dollars! Nevertheless, I had a mortgage to sustain (a mortgage that was solely in my name, bank loan and deed), and all the other innumerable bills to meet (again, all of them in my name). In this small town, it was impossible for me to hide what I was going through. I was struggling, so I'd resolved to sell the furniture in my home to make ends meet. This was when a coworker introduced me to this innovative concept of online yard sales, an introduction that would also lead me to a wonderful human being. I literally handed her my phone, and she created for me a Facebook account, stocked with all the most popular online yard sales surrounding Mullins and Kleb counties. In a matter of days, I'd sold nearly all the auxiliary furniture and decor within my home, making enough money to float my mortgage for two months.

Little did I know, however, that out of this moment—my intro to social media 101, my welcome to Facebook moment—would be birthed the friendship and love of a lifetime. I was sitting in my grandmother's living room, scrolling through my cousin's Facebook friends when I saw him. This particular cousin and I are only one year apart in age, to the month, so we'd often shared a number of mutual friends throughout our lives together. Still very new to Facebook and exploring beyond the scope of my online yard sales, I was eager to learn how to "friend" other people and catch up with those friends that I'd been forced to disconnect from. My thumb was in this dedicated, studious, upward motion when I quickly stopped... slowly pulled the page back downward, halting at the words, Ollie J Higdon. He was not a friend from my childhood, not even a familiar face. Yet, here I was, curious to know him. Eager to friend him.

True to form, I had my cousin private message this Ollie J Higdon. Two days later, this Ollie J Higdon responded to my third-party-dispatched message with a friend request. Our private messages evolved into texts that led to a phone call—that phone call laced with the butterflies of excitement and trepidation of the unknown. I was in Augusta, leaving Walmart with my "two little black boys," when Ollie and I first spoke on the phone. Ten digits popped up on the screen of my smart phone. In seconds, there was *hello* and the calm of his voice filled my atmosphere. I kept my cool, minus the ginormous smile on my face. (Thankfully, this Ollie J Higdon wasn't from planet Krypton and couldn't employ some X-ray vision to see through the phone.) I liked the raspiness of his voice... I liked the gentleness in his tone. I asked him something to the effect of how do you say your name... and he replied O-lly (pronounce like Holly minus the H) Higdun. This conversation was light, easy, fluid, fun. Something I definitely needed in wake of the overly strained, manipulative, abusive relationship with my estranged ex-husband. In a later conversation, Ollie and I had decided to meet—nothing heavy, nothing with commitment attached, nothing fancy, no expectations... just coffee. We both shared a thing for Starbucks coffee, so had decided to meet up at a local café. Ollie drove himself... I drove myself—nothing heavy, nothing with commitment attached, nothing fancy, no expectations... just coffee.

It's interesting—more like fascinating—when two grown folks have *a seat at the table,* grown folks with real jobs, real obligations, real issues, real struggles. There's this thing called *real talk* that unfolds. There's a difference between being an adult, being mature, and being grown. Grown folks have gone through and lived out some real shit and look at life from a different vantage point. Grown folks appreciate what they have and understand that the struggle is, indeed real, yet all the while necessary. So on this warm summer night sat two grown folks—transparent and real—engaged in real life and engaged in real talk. Ollie was sporting this lavender, short-sleeved polo, fresh from the dryer (in a good way... I mean, no hard creases to the sleeves, no stiff front and back) and dark wash jeans (no perfectly laundered crease... those, too, with that fresh-from-the-dryer relaxed vibe). His shoes didn't boast the luster of a fresh shoeshine. Instead, he sported a pair of gently worn earth-tone Steve Madden˚ lace-ups. His whole look was so relaxed, hell relaxing… something I'd certainly lost appreciation for while tethered to my covert aggressor. Meanwhile, I rocked a pair of light aqua blue shorts with a mustard v-neck relaxed fit short sleeve shirt. Red is one of my favorite colors so I'd accented my sea breeze look with my beloved red beaded necklace and topped off the fit with my dark-circles-under-the-eyes-hiding red glasses. I was cautiously nervous, but meeting him, being in Ollie's presence, seemed okay. This was not my first post-gaslighting date, and Mother Nature had surely taught me to listen to my instincts. This meeting with Ollie brought with it no alarming brushes with my history, no immediate red flags (not even a soft toot or low whistle). I'd been gaslighted for eight years, so I definitely knew what *Not Okay* felt like. This felt okay. I felt okay.

Ollie, nearly ten years my senior, had four children, and I, two sons. His children spanned an age group of uncharted territory for me, with the eldest age twenty-one and the youngest child eleven… my sons were four and two. Ollie and I took *a seat at the table* outside on the terrace. We opened in typical first date fashion, but immediately I was sure this Ollie was slightly atypical. After answering what it is I did for a living, I, of course in true first date fashion, reciprocated the question. Let's just say Ollie's response was candid, for sure, and definitely an icebreaker. The cleaner version of his response was that he specialized in underground utilities. I had absolutely noooo idea what this meant, so Ollie resolved to sum it up with his initial answer… he was a pipe layer. I laughed, and we carried on. Professionally, we were so different, but this thing called life had connected us.

Ollie and I talked about our pasts, and we particularly talked about my present. We talked about heavy, real issues like recreational activities (this is code for do you use or have ever used illicit drugs… do you have an addictive personality) and self-harm. Of course, we treaded lightly on the course of our past relationships but lent more energy to the paths not yet traveled. This was definitely a different interaction for me, something I'd not experienced in nearly ten years and something I'd definitely missed. The comfort of not being covertly challenged on all fronts; the peace of not having my thoughts twisted, manipulated; the joy of not being controlled and not having my words, decisions, and actions controlled. This was refreshing… not love at first sight or some shit from a fairy tale. There was no glass slipper, and I didn't believe this to be an instant *oh life was so messed up for you here's your happily ever after* moment. This, however, was real… real grown ups… real life unfolding before me… and definitely real talk. The only thing fake joining us at the table that night were the 14-inch Peruvian extensions shielding my very real bald crown. (And yes, our real talk involved talking about my not-even-close-to-real hair weave.)

Our soft laughter and conversation was brought to a silent halt with this expressionless look that suddenly fell upon Ollie's face. It wasn't the sharp, piercing, tight look of my ex-husband's countenance when I'd not met his standard. I'd have known that face. This face, however, was new to me, and I could not read its expression. From the looks of it, I wasn't sure if I should run or duck under the table as I attempted to trace Ollie's disposition. I'm thinking, oh my, an ex-girlfriend must be on the scene… *just okay* just turned into *absolutely not okay* (laughing out loud but not laughing in that moment). Two minutes later, however, there was the answer to Ollie's silence… a beautiful, olive-toned version of Ollie stood before us… it was his oldest daughter, Charlene. Talk about a first date (laughing out loud). Charlene had just gotten off work from this local seafood restaurant less than a quarter of a mile from our date night Starbucks'. She'd grabbed a cup of coffee with a friend and was exiting Starbucks® when she'd spotted her dad's midnight black F250. "Hello, I'm Charlene" were the words she spoke as she and I exchanged hellos for the first time. By now, all three of us had that "this is totally awkward" face on. Charlene explained she'd "slowly walked around the building" looking for her dad, as she knew that that was his truck and his location (courtesy of their GPS app) had showed him to be there. As quickly as she'd arrived at the table, Charlene was gone, with an "It was very nice meeting you" goodbye.

Moments later, we ended our evening just as it had began... Ollie walked me to my car. We exchanged a lighthearted hug and said goodbye. There was nothing heavy to our having met—nothing with commitment attached, nothing fancy, no expectations... just coffee and the roar from Ollie's truck as he exited left out of the parking lot. I was having one of my Ally McBeal moments, thinking, "Wow, that's not a good sign... he just floored it out of here... guess that didn't go too well" when my phone rang. It was Ollie. I was reluctant to answer, thinking (A) He's calling to dump me already, or (B)... I couldn't even process a B as I was too busy pining over option A. Nevertheless, I answered. To my surprise, my contemplations were all wrong. Ollie was calling to chitchat. He'd "had a good time" and had "really enjoyed meeting (me)." Here we were two grown folks kicking it like teenagers. I enjoyed his conversation and he, seemingly, enjoyed mine. That night, up had popped a text from this unknown number. It was Charlene and her kind words that would unknowingly mark the start of our friendship and mother-daughter relationship.

At a time when I'd had absolutely no business dating—I mean there was no therapist and I had not even begun the journey of reckoning with my story or healing from its truth—there we were. Ollie and I. Dating. Late night convos, peaceful strolls along the river, amazing dinners for two. We genuinely enjoyed being in the presence of one another. And as I'd seemingly lost everything to my covert aggressor and gaslighting, I'd embraced Ollie's friendship with a zeal to not have anything else taken from me—not my love for humanity, not my passion for life, not my love for love. I'd made a conscious decision not to allow my ex-husband to further control and dominate my life by me not dating or by me making the tragic mistake of lumping everyone into the same sick category as him. No, this mindset would not translate into me loosely dating, nor would it translate into me falling blindly in love with a pulse. This simply meant I would stay in tune with the Universe as I vowed to forever more be the captain of my own fate.

With Ollie, I had to have the courage to trust what had let me down before. I had to have courage…I had to have the courage to trust that one act of assertiveness that landed one disappointment did not mean every man would disappoint. I had to have the courage to know that what had resulted in one act of betrayal with my ex-husband did not mean that every relationship would end in this egregious act of betrayal. I had to have courage. After all, I was a long way from Lodebar. Once again in *my* life, I'd chosen to be vulnerable. I chose bravery over lies and courage over gaslighting. I'd chosen life and I'd chosen to live. I shared everything with Ollie, including (hell, especially) Greenleaf. Yep, this approach (being open, honest, vulnerable) had backfired before; but *this* wasn't before and I'd refused to be bound by and bound to my past. Together, Ollie and I chose to explore uncharted territories. And for those things we couldn't navigate alone, there was therapy.

What began as a private message and night of coffee grew into a beautiful, very real friendship and marriage. Ollie had even passed *the Grandma test*, as she was just as madly in love with him as was I, and very freely shared with Ollie the concerns she'd so privately held regarding my ex-husband. Seven months preceding the death of my world's greatest , Dolan Hudson, Ollie and I were joined in matrimony with only the pomp and circumstance of the love and happiness connecting us. There weren't eleven bridesmaids and thirteen groomsmen or a slew of guests. There wasn't some grand venue, decorated with the sweet fragrance of calla lilies. There was no groom's cake, no expensive catering, no lavish to dos. There was just the intimacy, love, and adoration for life shared by two grownups gathered in a judge's private chambers. There were no invitations and no stressful guest list—simply the joy of our children as witnesses to our moment... the hallmark of our story. And after a beautiful two-minute ceremony, my life partner and I enjoyed an intimate, fun dinner with our children. This new chapter in *our* story was unlike anything I could have ever imagined, yet so much more.

R.U.N.

My grandmother often said, "The Lord is better to us than we deserve," and in spite of previous hurts, in spite of the pains of my past, I was certain that in this Ollie J Higdon, the Lord had surely been better to me than I'd deserved. In the book of Isaiah, it is written, "Instead of your shame you will receive a double portion and instead of disgrace you will rejoice in your inheritance. And so you will also inherit a double portion in your land, and everlasting joy will be yours" (Isaiah 61:7) When I began the actual work of pinning down my journey (something that started as this enormous journal entry but evolved into this book), I was pregnant with my daughter, Olivia. Just 6 years earlier, I thought my life was over, that I'd never love, trust, breathe again … had even questioned if there was a God, and if so, why the hell had He let me go through so much pain. But here I am, very alive and very much so owning my story. I have come to understand that when we are hurt, physically, mentally, and emotionally driven to the point of isolation—when we become *that* island—we can be certain that the island will provide. And instead of perpetual agony, disappointment, and shame, God's panacea rests in *that* double portion and everlasting joy. Today, I bounce around with this joy that people still don't understand. I have no shame, as my life speaks as a testament to what it truly means to bounce back and operate every day, from a place of forgiveness, compassion, and pure faith.

Today, my double portion and everlasting joy lives out loud in the form of the seven incredible children I am blessed with. At fourteen months old, Miss Olivia Grace is the youngest. As this bright-eyed little girl explores the world, I try to make that discovery as painless as possible. I caution her against those things that can harm her, and I teach her about everything else. As she smiles at her own image while waddling towards the oven, I warn her of the oven's unseen heat in hopes that she never gets burned. As she rolls carefree across my king size bed, I meet her at the opposite side to warn her of the nasty fall that quietly awaits. On our walks through the neighborhood, I speak to Olivia about the beauty of the Universe, from the color of the trees to the wonder of the alligator snapping turtle, sunbathing alongside the lake. It is my duty to teach Olivia.

But then there is this thing called gaslighting. Like the heat from the oven, it is oftentimes unseen yet burns all the same. There's this mystery in its inconspicuous nature and power in its silence. So how do I protect my child from such a treacherous beast? Do I wait to meet her at the opposite side to help pick up the pieces after she's rolled blindly through life and taken a crippling fall, or do I stand tall in the face of this looming giant and speak to gaslighting for what it is? To all of my children, daughters *and* sons, what would I say to warn them of this danger that looms in the distance in hopes that their safety is maintained? I searched my soul to find the words that I'd wished someone had spoken to me. It was in these secret moments of meditation that I listened to God... not talked to Him ... listened. The revelation was quite simple – R.U.N.!

Before therapy, before this definition for the hell I'd been privately living, there was my God and I (and I alone) knew what He had spoken into my spirit and over my life. When

I was face down in the arena, marred and definitely failing, I had all sorts of opinions offered up over my situation. God had compelled me to move back home, in spite of the fact that this would mean leaving parts of me behind in Lodebar. In return, He'd asked only that I trust Him. By no means was this a simple proclamation. Nevertheless, this was what He had spoken into my spirit and over my life, and I would, by all means, comply. What I found most interesting, however, was how this was perceived by people of my shared faith and beliefs. One of the deacons from my church even told me, "You can't run from this." Only he had no idea what the hell "this" was and no appreciation for what it means to R.U.N. This deacon had not lived *my* trauma, he had not been gaslighted, and he had not heard from *my* God as I had. I am reminded by Brené Brown that "we need to be selective about the feedback we let into our lives".[51] Don't allow other people, especially those that have not lived and breathed your trauma, to make pronouncements over your life. While these people are sitting back, passing their own judgments, forecasting their own predictions upon your life, I implore you to remember that to R.U.N. does not always speak to running from something but, ultimately, running towards something … something more hopeful than that which defines your past. When God speaks to you and commands you to move, get your ass in high gear and in the metaphorical sense of this word, R.U.N.!

I'd survived pharmacy school by using these little crafty thought processes called mnemonic devices, so it was of no wonder God would land me such a poignant one to use as a tool to empower my daughters and the sons and daughters of this world. (Yes, He does have a sense of humor!)

Recognize something's wrong, even if you don't know exactly what the *something* is. Having not grown up with a cohesive set of parents by which to model my life, I thought my husband's behaviors were normal and our way of marriage to be normal. Know that if you're operating with a covert-aggressive personality, there is no moral crisis of the conscience. "Reinforce the idea in your mind that the manipulator is merely fighting for something".[52] You must "redefine the terms of engagement" in order to survive this style of fighting and level of skilled abuse.[53] Perform your own litmus test and have a trusted friend or therapist help with analyzing the results. Don't simply dismiss questionable behavior or repeat patterns of behavior as the norm or as acceptable. Listen to that tiny whisper within that speaks volumes! And when that whisper roars with answers, don't follow through with a million different questions. Don't ask why, or how, what if, or what next. Simply follow the command.

My bonus son, Jerry, is an incredible football player, playing on both the offensive and defensive lines. I met Jerry when he was eleven and, have since, learned a lifetime about football. One of the most intriguing aspects of football is all of the various positions the players assume and what these positions represent. When Jerry's on the O-line (offensive line), he takes the field in this crouched down, three-point stance. His knees are bent (in a squat position), back slightly inclined forward, left arm cocked to his hip region, right hand touching the ground, and his head raised, facing his opponent. As an offensive guard, this physical stance gives Jerry power, an explosive start in response to the play… leverage against his opponent. When the play is over, the offensive line scurries off the field and huddles under this canopy where a television has already been set up and the team can review each play. The team takes this moment to strategize, critique where things went wrong, and build on the fruitful actions. The players get guidance from their coach and set off, back to the field, more impactful and better equipped to execute. Here's my point: when you're in this game called life and the play is over … you've identified that you've been gaslighted … and you hustle off the field to regroup, I encourage you to huddle up with your squad (be this a therapist, friends, family, or spiritual connect) and replay, aloud, the conversations and questionable moments etched in your memory. If in this huddle you discover that your adversary constantly offers up all these *alternate versions* of the truth, I challenge you to get down in that three-point stance—knees bent, head raised high, staring your opponent square in the face—and R.U.N.!

Usurp his authority by maintaining your own! "Take your own independent, assertive stand".[54] To be clear, I mean launch a full-scale mutiny! Protecting yourself from the insidious effects of gaslighting is key to your very survival. Gaslighters have an appetite for human destruction and demoralization. A person that willingly engages in this behavior will stop at nothing shy of your demise. "Making headway in conflicts with aggressive and covertly aggressive personalities…can only happen when you're willing to invest your time and energy where you have unquestionable power: your own behavior".[55] So if you have to give up *everything* to restore all of you, boldly do so! "Be strong and courageous. Do not be afraid or terrified because of them, for the Lord your God goes with you; He will never leave you nor forsake you" (Deuteronomy 31:6) Avoid the quagmire of assuming the gaslighter will miraculously change. In the mind of the gaslighter, he is not wrong but always right! It is a losing battle trying to make the manipulator change.[56]

Take, for instance, the following scenario. Imagine you've just arrived at your favorite restaurant. You've been anticipating this moment all day… at work thinking about this amazing dinner, deep in thought chatting it up with your favorite server and mapping out what to order. The ambience at this restaurant is incredible! The warm dim lighting, the soothing music, the luxurious colors. And the service, impeccable. The attendant greets you with a warm smile and seats you. You're glancing over the menu, awaiting your favorite server, when this complete stranger approaches the table. Dressed in the appropriate uniform, this person asks for your drink order and casually provides you the evening's specials. Already thrown off by the unfamiliar presence, you resolve to order your customarily favorite dish. You order your ribeye medium-well with a side of buttery steamed broccoli and rich fingerling potatoes. Minutes later, the server returns. Instead of your perfectly prepared steak, he places a platter of emotional distress on the table with a hearty side of psychological manipulation. Instead of those richly flavored fingerling potatoes, you find yourself glaring at a hefty portion of gaslighting. You question the server, but he assures you that the meal sitting before you is exactly what you ordered. With great pause and immense reservation, you think of what to do next. Do you remain? Do you succumb to this server's explanations? Do you eat from a meal you didn't order? Or do you stand to your feet, assert your position, and walk away? Absolute power rests in your own behavior.[57]

Never mind the naysayers. I once heard it said, "Beware of distractions." A distraction can set you off course, disrupt things, create imbalance. Gaslighting, in and of itself, is this colossal distraction that will keep you more than preoccupied. Not to mention the overt distraction offered in the mere existence of the gaslighter. So there is absolutely not a single solitary minutia of time or irrecoverable expenditure of energy to devote to the appeal of this captivating audience of naysayers. Their opinions, their voice, their platform, their existence is not important. To be clear, however, their purpose is, and that purpose is to replete you, to keep you grounded, and to keep you focused on you! In actuality, these naysayers are like a little battery pack or your own personal power source, when, by design, they're goal is to short-circuit your network. Funny how the Universe works.

Never mind the whisper campaign, particularly when it's an alliance made up of the people closest to you, the ones that claim they love you. There will always be those individuals rallying to see you fail. "Personal emotional attacks made by people not engaged in problem-solving have zero value in building or creating anything – they're only an attempt to tear down and invalidate what others are attempting to build".[58] These critics are simply a non-factor. Never mind them and their "cheap-seat criticism".[59] These critics are inconsequential with the exceptional purpose of keeping you focused on your goal.

I absolutely love music, so I engage in lots of time aimed at simply listening to the lyrics, oftentimes finding a direct link to these words and my life. I tend to caution people that the genre of music I'm listening to, all the way down to the artist and lyrics, usually speaks to my emotional state and true feelings dancing around in my spirit. That is, if I'm really not feeling an individual, situation, or time and place, I can be sure to express myself by dialing into a song that speaks for me … somewhat like the transformer that speaks through music. So while listening to one of my favorite artists, this amazing song came to mind as I thought about the attributes akin to the covert-aggressor, gaslighters, and this incredibly negative group of individuals I call naysayers. I've found the lyrics of Sara Bareilles' *King of Anything*[60] to epitomize the mind and spirit driving this group.

You've got opinions, man
We're all entitled to 'em, but I never asked
So let me thank you for your time,
And try not to waste anymore of mine
And get out of here fast

I hate to break it to you, babe, but I'm not drowning
There's no one here to save

Who cares if you disagree?
You are not me
Who made you king of anything?
So you dare tell me who to be?
Who died and made you king of anything?

You sound so innocent, all full of good intent
Swear you know best
But you expect me to jump up on board with you
And ride off into your delusional sunset

I'm not the one who's lost with no direction
But you'll never see
You're so busy making masks with my name on them in all caps
You got the talking down, just not the listening

And so on with the refrain. I've coined this song Team
Haters, Team Not Important, Team Negativity, Team Naysayer's
anthem. Lastly, **Never** give up on the journey of healing and
the power of loving yourself again! I have discovered that this
is the most challenging aftermath of unabated exposure to
gaslighting. "Remember, the tactics covert-aggressives use are
effective tools of impression-management".[61] The aggressor's
past behavior is most predictive of what is to come, and again,

this disturbed personality is not interested in change. What's more is that the thought of losing is nowhere on his [the covert-aggressor's] radar. Therefore you must stay grounded and centered on what lies ahead and never lose this footing.

Dr. Simon cautions that when operating with the covert-aggressive personality, "take appropriate action to protect yourself" and "secure a strong support system".[62] For some individuals, family, friends, and the supernatural powers of prayer come to mind when one mentions support systems. I, for one, had been raised up to pray about everything, and the dealings with my covert-aggressor were not exempt. My grandmother would tell me that God operates through prayer and fasting. When you pray, she'd proffer, you talk to God and when you fast, God speaks to you. I'd been praying and I'd been fasting. However, out there on the battlefield of life, getting my ass kicked, and losing at every stop, I've learned that sometimes the Lord doesn't answer these prayers in some overt, booming voice. Sometimes He answers in the most peculiar way, including through therapy. Sometimes, God leads you to a Google search that lands you a kick-ass therapist that helps you dust off the debris, adjust your armor, and teaches you how to fight!

For me the strong support system Dr. Simon writes about presented itself in the form of my family *and* therapist. According to Dr. Simon, many victims of gaslighting "have reported being stymied in their rehabilitation when seeking help from a professional not familiar enough with such severe forms of emotional abuse and the traumatic impact it can have on a person's psyche".[63] He goes on to say that those that have experienced "prolonged or intense gaslighting often need specialized help".[64] Never shy away from seeking professional or specialized help when navigating through life with a gaslighter. My individual and group sessions with my therapist provided me a safe and healthy space to share my trauma and to learn from the journey of others. There's this innate power and strength in identifying when the very fabric of your integrity has been compromised, and there is even greater hope in knowing that this breach can be mended. With the tireless help of my support system, I found the courage of my conviction to speak up for myself, be assertive, set boundaries, and fight for what was left of me. When grappling with the manipulative personality, never rescind your power and know that in standing your ground, there *is* light at the end of the tunnel. True light. Know that you shall be whole again.

Epilogue

I was still trying to figure out all the new folds, creases, and tiger marks of my six-month post cesarean body when Charlene, my oldest bonus daughter, came to me with this fabulous idea that we run a 5K together. Seriously, this had always been one of my personal life goals. I've always been into working out, and I actually enjoy running, so the thought of doing a 5K has always been a BFD for me (Big Fitness Deal). However, right here, right now, at this very moment, my body was like *What?!?!* I think *she* may have fainted for a moment, and I may have had to bring *her* back (*she and her* being the part of me that totally freaked the hell out). I'd spent the four months preceding Olivia's birth on bed rest, so this advanced maternal age body was way away from even its baseline. This request, however, was a request from my daughter, and I dare not let her down. I let all these "*We should do what?!?!*" thoughts skateboard through my mind (and yes, a few slipped out of my mouth) as I happily committed to our mother-daughter 5K.

The 5K was not until March, so I would spend the next couple of months training. Whether it was on the elliptical, biking, or hitting the pavement in the neighborhood, Olivia and I were on it! Come the big day, I was ready! I'd dropped a few pounds, bought all the right equipment, and had mentally prepared myself for the challenge. I was so excited! Excited to be doing something I'd always wanted to do, excited to be doing it at my age, and most excited to be doing so alongside Charlene. God had blessed me with two Amazing bonus daughters that challenged me to be great, and this feat was evidence of just that! Charlene is this total fitness guru, so just seconds before the race began, I thought it best to forewarn her that it was totally okay if she left me. I was amongst good company as the race had sold out! I would just see her at the finish line. We did our thumbs up, and the race began! Yep, in seconds, Charlene was gone, and this bonus mom was trucking along with the sea of people, walkers and runners alike.

I ran the first two miles plus some nonstop. Thought, not bad for this mama! Besides, this was my first time running without a stroller in front of me. That last three-quarters of the final mile, however, were pure torture! I kept thinking someone had to have made this mile longer. Surely, someone had moved the trail. I'd run, walk, run, walk again. Finally, I was just sure I simply could not run, not even a single step more. There were small groups stationed along the trail to cheer us runners on ... to help keep us going ... but I just couldn't. This mama was done.

At this point of assenting surrender, I've got my music bumpin', and I'm walking, my Brooks' all dusty from the red clay dirt trail. I'm solo power pumping it around this bend, which leads up this steep hill, when out of nowhere comes this young girl. She must have been fourteen or fifteen years old, dark blonde hair pulled up in a ponytail, and she's screaming, "Come On! You Can Do This! You're Almost There! Come On!" I hear this young girl clear as the music coming through my Beats! Not only is she screaming these words to me, but she's pumping her fist and breaks out running, all the while screaming, "Come On!" I immediately start running with her! I forgot how tired I was. Forgot that I could hear my heart beating in my head! All I could hear was this young girl screaming "Come On! You Can Do This!" and there she was running *with* me. And she didn't just jumpstart the run, take a few steps with me, then stop, and turn back. She ran up this full steep hill with me! I nearly cried! All the while, this girl kept right on encouraging me, saying, "You're Almost There!" The beautiful thing is that at the top of that steep hill was the bridge connecting the trail to the finish line. She was right. I was almost there. I was so tired, so fatigued by the excitement and actuality of the run that I'd lost sight of the finish line. See, this 5K ended where it had begun. It should have been easy for me to remember the course. But with all the people, the newness of the moment, the exhilaration of the experience in and of itself, I'd lost sight. I'd lost sight of my goal, but not for long. Someone had already been placed in position, set up on the sideline to champion me, to shout over the noise, to overpower the fatigue, and help me continue on my way.

There's this exhilarating feeling in stepping into the arena voluntarily, knowingly, on your own terms. But when face down in the arena, an arena you've been thrown into—an arena you've not signed up for, not trained for, not conditioned for—the feeling isn't quite the same. For me, gaslighting was that unwarranted arena, and this is what I've learned from it. In this life, you will be tried, tested. And yes, you will absolutely find your ass stumbling, marred, and coming up way short. Know that the victory lies in staying true to yourself and standing firm in your beliefs. Brené writes that irrespective of our spiritual traditions, "our faith narratives must be protected".[65] This I do believe. It is in the trenches of these life tests, these moments of absolute failure, that it seems easy to lose hope, to doubt God's plan or purpose for your life... maybe question if even there is a God. Whatever God looks like to you, however God speaks to you, I ask that you hold fast! When your hope meter is depleted, hold fast! Hope is this operative word that represents faith in motion. When you're tired, exasperated by your race, hope meets you on the sideline and helps you finish what you began. "Hope is a function of struggle".[66] So in those darkest, most painful moments, when all hope is seemingly gone, I ask you to remember the power in your struggle and know that you were placed in this very unique position for such a time as this (Esther 4:14). I believe there are no mistakes in this life and we are all destined for purpose. Instead of asking why God allowed something painful or tragic to happen *to* you, ask what wondrous feat God has allowed to happen *through* you. Just maybe God has set you upon a platform to deliver His people from something horrific, like the silent emotional and psychological bondage of gaslighting. Maybe *through* you, lives will be saved or forever transformed. Maybe, just maybe, *through* you, someone's daughter or son will be emboldened enough to break the fierce grip of silence and speak out about their own abuse.

I am reminded of this simplification I was once offered up in learning the different dynamics that govern grammar. We've all studied conjunctions and how these words are integral in connecting phrases or sentences. The conjunction can essentially set the tone of the sentence, depending upon its type (e.g., coordinating, subordinating, correlative). In our daily communications, we tend to toss around this little three letter coordinating conjunction that, when spoken or written, typically shifts the context of the entire subject matter towards an unfavorable end. This tiny word, *but*, inherently has the power to redirect our thinking, our actions, our end. By design, the word *but* creates contrast. My challenge to you is to meditate on a positive contrast. Redefine the narrative and all that follows the word *but*. Greenleaf was meant to destroy me, *but* what the enemy had intended for harm worked together for good (Genesis 50:20). *But* for that place in time, I am here. Now, I appreciate and understand that which was created for me to despise.

I've been in the arena for quite some time. The fight is far from easy and will likely never be over. The difference is I am now smarter and far better equipped for warfare. Thanks to my therapist, I now have these *special skills* that help me strive valiantly in the arena. These principles shape the core of my being and help me to survive the everyday challenges afforded on this journey. Here's some of what I've learned in therapy, invaluable skills that have helped me arrive at *this* place:

To know your enemy is to know their fighting style. This knowledge is power and may very well be the one thing that saves your life. My enemy – this covert-aggressor. His fighting style – gaslighting. With this information, the arena is no longer this daunting force but more like a marathon I'm training for.

I set boundaries by which I communicate and operate. I practice mindfulness, living in the moment…cherishing that moment, especially with my kids. Meditation and prayer go hand in hand for me, and I actively engage in the art of self-care. I am a master at the practice of shame resilience as parts that are dearest to me are still exposed, damn near daily, to gaslighting. For these parts, it is imperative that I not sit in a state of negative energy, yet rest comfortably in the positive realm of shame resilience.

I have diffusers all over the place for what I call subliminal therapy, to silence those parts of me that are curiously poking around the hornet's nest when I need them to stand down. I even have extras stowed away in the event that my workhorses burn out (after all, they do put in a lot of work). And likewise, there's water therapy, and I do mean darn near any kind of water—running water, trickling water, a fountain, a lake, a hot bath, the ocean (I think you get the point.) It's not uncommon for me to employ one or both of these tools while exercising one of my greatest devices, journaling.

Journaling is my freest and most freeing form of expression and release (okay, more so tied with working out). Journaling has taught me that while you have to be cautious of what others speak over your life, you must be equally aware of your self-talk. I've found it helpful to leave Post-it® notes throughout my personal spaces, short messages to keep me grounded and encouraged. And when that's not enough, I practice something called self-text. I have ordained myself the queen of text messages. I really don't like to talk on the phone, but I absolutely love to text. I often send those I love and care about text messages to uplift them and let them know I care. So why not do the same for myself. When the temperature rises and shit really hits the fan, I shoot myself a text message, a quick reminder that everything will be okay, or to simply breathe. When a little more oomph is required to capture the fullness of the moment, I pop open the notes section within my phone and allow my fingers to run wild.

"To know thyself is to know wisdom" (Socrates). Know your enemy. *Check.* Know thyself. *Double check.* To know this new version of myself was to embrace, not ignore or hide, my trauma and to recognize (as well as appreciate) the parts of me that were still struggling. To really know and understand myself required another assignment. August 2017, my therapist introduced me to *Parts Work* and this therapy model that looks at Internal Family Systems (IFS). As with every other book Julie has recommended that I read, I offer this read to anyone seeking to better understand what makes them tick. My initial, in-my-head-response to Julie's description of "parts" and "the Self" was something to the effect of "*Oh no, she's telling me I have multiple personalities.*" Retrospectively, after having read the book, I can imagine all of my parts racing to the living room—some rockin' red specs, some in purple glasses, a few in black frames, others plain face, all with shoulders shrugged and this look of total confusion and frustration—trying to figure out where these other personalities were and then, where the hell their parts were (you'll get it once you read the book). Julie quickly calmed the living room with her continued explanation of *Parts Work*. Here's my takeaway.

What if we—the fascinating beings each of us are uniquely created to be—what if we are indeed the sum total of our *parts*? Just two years before my very own Wonder Woman came onto the scene, Sigmund Freud, in his brilliance, postulated that the human mind is intricately compromised of systems that work together to create our personalities. Without going too deep into his work, Freud posited that the psyche is compromised of the id (our genetic, instinctual part), ego (our realistic part), and the super-ego (our moral compass or conscious part). Decades later, this family therapist Richard Schwartz, Ph.D., expounded on Freud's school of thought with his Internal Family Systems (IFS) model. This model presented a new approach to individual therapy and drew on constructs from the family (as this organized entity with different players playing different roles) merged with this idea of what many psychologists refer to as subpersonalities or ego states.[67] In the book *Parts Work*, Holmes uses these very realistic (and for me, very relatable) illustrations to explore Schwartz's IFS model.

"The term 'parts' refers to the experience of having shifting states of mind that have unique sets of thoughts, feelings and behaviors".[68] According to Schwartz, this is not a transient emotional state but instead a discrete, autonomous mental system that has an "idiosyncratic range of emotion, style of expression, and set of abilities, intentions, or functions".[69] "Each part has a job in our system" and each part plays a critical role in balancing the internal human system. It is our parts that make us compassionate, make us tear up at that heart-gripping scene in a movie, make us clutch our keys when crossing a half-lit parking lot at night, make us worry over those abstract things that are out of our control. Our parts are in play when that no-you-didn't part wants to fly off with a text in response to something inflammatory; yet the not-a-good-idea manager halts the keystrokes. It's one of our parts that throws up the middle finger to the driver that sharply cut us off, and there's another part that takes center to explain to the three-year-old sitting in the backseat what that not-so-wonderful gesture means. In some fashion or another, we've all had those moments when we can say, "a part of me...." These parts are real and lend humanity a shared connection. It is our parts that are created as we grow and wade through the waters of this thing called life. Our parts arise out of necessity "to help us adapt to physical, psychological, and social needs".[70] And though at times not self-evident, our parts are created for positive intention, even when that part exhibits a behavior or emotion that promotes a seemingly negative or adverse consequence. In short, our parts are "designed to help us cope with the tasks of living".[71]

The "Self" is the "centered place of consciousness where we can witness or observe these 'parts' or patterns of thoughts and feeling we are experiencing".[72] "When we are in the state of consciousness we call the Self, we are able to observe the parts but are not taken over by them".[73] The Self represents the core of who we are and is "characterized by mindful awareness, compassionate connectedness, and calm, confident clarity".[74] The Self sits back and observes our parts, a concept my brain translated as a bit of a watchful eye, while "Buddhists refer to it as the 'witness' or 'mindfulness'".[75]

I've always been a visual learner, so my favorite part of this book is Holmes' representation of what "parts" and "Self" look like. Holmes creates this "picture" of the inner world by graphically depicting a Buddhist perspective on the nature of consciousness as presented by Vietnamese Buddhist monk, Thich Nhat Hanh.[76] Thich Nhat Hanh uses a circle to depict the two important levels of consciousness. At the bottom half of the circle we find the "store consciousness," our "regularly occurring states of mind" referred to as our parts.[77] "The top half of the circle represents our everyday consciousness, what Thich Nhat Hanh calls the 'living room' of our consciousness".[78] According to Buddhist psychology, "when internal and external conditions support a part being in the living room of the everyday mind it will rise up; when the conditions no longer support it, it will go back down into storage" [store consciousness].[79] This concept made so much sense to me! When I'm hangry (hungry and angry at the same time), I could envision my hangry part rising up from that lower part of the circle, blasting into the living room, kicking over shit, dialed all the way up over food. And, once the external condition no longer supports hanger (i.e., I've eaten), that part returns to store consciousness. Needless to say, I laughed, several times, as I navigated through this book, visibly seeing my many parts at work.

The objective of parts work or IFS therapy is to help us identify and understand our parts as well as learn how to effectively engage the Self for those rigid, extreme, or overly active parts. This skill helps us to heal and balance our internal system. In his work, Schwartz identified common roles for parts that existed across people. These three distinct parts are managers, exiles, and firefighters.[80] The managers arise out of necessity to keep the individual functional and safe. These parts are seemingly analytical and very astute, surveying the internal and external environments for potential stressors and quickly developing a plan of action to protect the system. "When a person has been hurt, humiliated, frightened, or shamed in the past, he or she will have parts that carry the emotions, memories, and sensations from those experiences. Managers often want to keep these feelings out of consciousness and, consequently, try to keep vulnerable, needy parts locked in inner closets. These incarcerated parts are known as exiles".[81] Whenever an exile is upset to a level that it threatens to release an overpowering emotion into the system, the firefighter is thrust into the living room of consciousness.[82] "This group tries to douse the inner flames of feeling as quickly as possible".[83] Much like the manager parts, the firefighters strive to protect the system.

In reading this book, I understood that there was not a part of me that had not been impacted by gaslighting. Not a single part left untouched. There was the part of me, that intuitive part, that had risen up into the living room of my consciousness and commanded that I run when I sat, buckled in with fear in the car at Dr. Smith's office. Yet at the same time, my everything-is-gonna-be-okay part (the gaslighted placator) echoed the sentiments of my abuser, so I'd remained. I now understand my manager part put in overtime to keep everything in order, to correct much of the turbulence she'd attributed to my eager-to-please part. The manager blamed the accommodating and compromising parts for us being in this predicament to start with. Meanwhile, my anxious parts flooded the living room with worry and panic. And there was my spiritual part encouraging prayer and steadfast hope while the little devil with the pitchfork part said, "To hell with that."

My parts danced all over the place trying to grasp the introduction of this thing called gaslighting into their space. But the part most impacted, most triggered, most ignited by this abuse was my child part. This part took over the living room, often times screaming, "Get the hell out!" to everyone else. This part was pretty powerful as she brought with her a litany of emotions including fear, exponential panic, anger, and rage that, once dissipated, resulted in tears, sorrow, shame, sadness, and sometimes exhaustion. When this child part entered the living room, the space around me would spin. If this part took to the living room of my core during session, I could hear my therapist speaking but could not follow her words. I could feel my breathing speed up, hear each beat of my heart amplify. This sensation was not the equivalence of a panic attack. It was different and scary. It was the same child part of me that had taken over the living room as my involuntary committal was handed down. Only after I'd admitted to Julie that this room-spinning-phenomena was happening (and happening often in and out of sessions) could we honor this part, figure out what it was she needed, and help her balance the inner system.

This child part had been abandoned and failed by both of her parents, had been abused, had been sexually assaulted. And the trauma of gaslighting had pulled her, this miniature incredible hulk-like child part forward to protect the system. Her own traumas had instilled in her this fury that longed to protect the self. Though it was too little too late, the child part was very present and always trying to rectify the breach. This child part needed to be unburdened[84] and what she needed was simple – to be held and to be told, to be reassured, that everything is okay. To be apologized to for the shortcomings of her parents and trauma of her youth and to know that her adult part was front and center and taking care of her and all the other parts. She desperately needed to know that she was okay.

Gaslighting is psychological warfare, and as is the case with training and conditioning for any battle, my therapist taught me to listen to my body and respond accordingly. All of my parts and all of my emotions are important and must be validated as I move through this continuum of healing and restoration. Julie encouraged me to acknowledge these parts compassionately, but "not sit in" their emotional state. Acknowledge the sting but don't sit in it. Acknowledge the fatigue, but don't sit in it. Acknowledge the pain, but don't sit in it. To sit in it is to surrender, and I didn't come this far to just give up. Through parts work, I learned how to identify the parts of me that were greatly imbalanced by gaslighting. We worked through some of these more rigid parts, providing them with the tools they needed to be more effective in my internal family system. My therapist helped me to further understand my triggers and cope with the aftermath of my gaslighting, this mental health infraction called PTSD (post-traumatic stress disorder).

Every day, I live with the post-traumatic stress of my abuser's disorder. Every day. Sometimes the stress of my abuser's disorder plays out in common day-to-day interactions, and at other times, it violently manifests itself in the lives of my "two little black boys." The trauma of gaslighting was personally so big for me—so overwhelming—that it had tapped into (triggered) other parts and other traumas (like when your sibling runs up to you singing, *Oooh you're in trouble,* and you ask *Big trouble or little trouble?*). Gaslighting was akin to big trouble, and now there were these little troubles, preexisting traumas, stirred up with it. My second day at Greenleaf, I'd learned there were no cameras in the hall on which my room was located. My room was the second room on the right, distal to the hall entrance. These were coed quarters, and there obviously were no locks on the doors. Out of fear of ever being sexually assaulted again, fear of ever reliving such trauma, each night I'd wrap myself in the three hospital blankets the staff had provided me. The first blanket I'd wrapped left to right; the second blanket right to left; and the last blanket in the opposite direction. I figured at best, I'd feel my attacker trying to move through the mummy-like wrapping of blankets. Now, I sleep under two heavy blankets with anywhere from two to three pillows stacked upon my feet. This creates a weighted sensation and I, in turn, feel safe.

I do not own or wear white socks. In all my hard work, processing and healing, this still remains one of my greatest triggers. I nearly fainted in a local retail store when my oldest son, age seven, so casually asked me to buy him a pack of crew-style athletic *white socks*. The space around me began to spin, and I could hardly breathe. I grabbed the socks out of the small black cart and gently nudged my son to get the multi-colored pack. Nevertheless, my big guy insisted on those damn white socks. So there we were… my internal barometer broken by the intensity of the moment… my hands clammy, armpits wet, and forehead covered with sweat beads as I glared at those white socks.

And there was the ultimate trigger. That trigger I could not escape. That trigger I could not pray away, wish away, diffuse away. It was sure to rear its head whether I liked it or not. There was no sidestepping Father Time. Whether I liked it or not, each year I was guaranteed to face this demon, the anniversary of Greenleaf. I loathed August 15th. Yet, I'd unknowingly thought of all the many ways to purposefully mourn its arrival. I'd take that day off from work, just to marvel at its pain. I'd soak in my bathtub on that day, basking in the beauty of my trauma. I'd stare at *that* date on the calendar, like piercing eyes would change the inevitable.

In therapy, I am reminded that some things will never be the same, as in the way they were before my ex-husband, before the covert-aggressor, before gaslighting. Likewise, I am reminded that this is okay. My therapist did, however, offer me this amazing strategy for how to deal with or assuage the evil little bastards (triggers) as they surface in my life. Her technique was simple, profound. "Replace existing file." Julie likened this statement to the warning box that typically pops up when you're saving a document. The computer software is designed to warn you that a file already exists with the selected title. If you've already saved the file under an original header and attempt to save the file again, the computer usually asks if you wish to replace the existing file. One would imagine the newer, edited version of the file to be better, or more refined, than the previous edition. After all, in replacing the existing file, you've created something new. And while this file might hold some of the data (or life experiences, if you will) from the previous file, it is a new thing (Isaiah 43:19). In silencing my triggers, in braving my PTSD, in moving to *that* place called purpose, it was imperative that I replace the existing file.

While some people wish to never remember what happened to them, I pray never to forget! To forget is to silence my truth, to disavow my story, and abandon the woman in the white socks. To forget is to lend gaslighting its most powerful platform, and that simply ain't gonna happen … not on my watch. EVERY DAY is a new day for me. It is an opportunity for me to share my truth, inspire others to be bold and brave, and to totally muck up the orchestrated game plan of the covert-aggressor and this abusive tactic called gaslighting. The evolution of my journey to doing what Brené Brown calls *Rising Strong* is best reflected here in her Manifesto of the Brave and Brokenhearted:[85]

There is no greater threat to the critics
and cynics and fearmongers
Than those of us who are willing to fall
Because we have learned how to rise

With skinned knees and bruised hearts;
We choose owning our stories of struggle,
Over hiding, over hustling, over pretending.

When we deny our stories, they define us.
When we run from struggle, we are never free.
So we turn toward truth and look it in the eye.

We will not be characters in our stories.
Not villains, not victims, not even heroes.

We are the authors of our lives.
We write our own daring endings.

We craft love from heartbreak,
Compassion from shame,
Grace from disappointment,
Courage from failure.

Showing up is our power.
Story is our way home.
Truth is our song.
We are the brave and brokenhearted.
We are rising strong.

Today, I stand *next* to the woman in the white socks and
help her to rise strong. For those of you that have had the
courage to work through your trauma, you can appreciate the

beauty of standing *next to* but not *in* that body of trauma. I can see the woman in the white socks, sporting a beautiful navy blue, green, and white maxi dress. I can see the sprouts of hair budding from her unshaven legs. I can smell the scent of her lotion and smooth the edges of her hair. Most importantly, I can talk to her, calm her, and encourage her… all the while standing *next to* her. Now, I remind her, "You are one bad chick! You are not crazy! You are a damn great mom! Bump that, you are a powerhouse, all-star kick ass mom! Great just ain't enough! You are a good person, the granddaughter of Dolan Hudson, engineered to love greatly, wired to actually give a shit, crafted to persevere."

The woman in the white socks, I honor her struggles, I honor her trauma, I honor her pain. From the sideline, running next to her, I champion her for simply having the tenacity to show up. I champion her trials. I champion her cause. I champion her truth. When she's tired, I tell her it's okay to take a break; it's okay to slow down, but to never give up. When she finds herself face planted in the dusty arena, I help her to rise strong, again and again. And when the critics try to tear her down with their empty words and honest lies, I yell out from the sideline, R.U.N.! and remind her that the gain in the R.U.N. is big enough to swallow up the agony of the process. When those shysty players like guilt, shame, anger, defeat, and fear enter the arena, I stand tall next to the woman in the white socks and remind her to not lend them a foothold. I walk *next to* her, down the hallways of Greenleaf, back to *day two*, back to *that* chair, back to *that* moment. Only this time, we don't randomly flip through the Book of Psalms. We are now of much greater focus … more grounded … more connected … more deliberate in our intent. We purposefully turn to Psalm 27, where the woman in the white socks is reminded of God's boundless faithfulness.

[1] The Lord is my light and my salvation—
  whom shall I fear?
The Lord is the stronghold of my life—
  of whom shall I be afraid?
[2] When the wicked advance against me
  to devour me,
it is my enemies and my foes
  who will stumble and fall.
[3] Though an army besiege me,
  my heart will not fear;
though war break out against me,
  even then I will be confident.
[4] One thing I ask from the Lord,
  this only do I seek:
that I may dwell in the house of the Lord
  all the days of my life,
to gaze on the beauty of the Lord
  and to seek him in his temple.
[5] For in the day of trouble
  he will keep me safe in his dwelling;
he will hide me in the shelter of his sacred tent
  and set me high upon a rock.
[6] Then my head will be exalted
  above the enemies who surround me;
at his sacred tent I will sacrifice with shouts of joy;
  I will sing and make music to the Lord.
[7] Hear my voice when I call, Lord;
  be merciful to me and answer me.
[8] My heart says of you, "Seek his face!"
  Your face, Lord, I will seek.
[9] Do not hide your face from me,
  do not turn your servant away in anger;
  you have been my helper.

Do not reject me or forsake me,
  God my Savior.
¹⁰ Though my father and mother forsake me,
  the Lord will receive me.
¹¹ Teach me your way, Lord;
  lead me in a straight path
  because of my oppressors.
¹² Do not turn me over to the desire of my foes,
  for false witnesses rise up against me,
  spouting malicious accusations.
¹³ I remain confident of this:
  I will see the goodness of the Lord
  in the land of the living.
¹⁴ Wait for the Lord;
  be strong and take heart
  and wait for the Lord.

I pay homage to the woman in white socks ... to her courage and her strength to be brave. Every day we write our own daring ending. In hopes that you never stand *in* my white socks, I share my truth.

———⸻———

I tell you this so that no one may deceive you by fine-sounding arguments. For though I am absent from you in body, I am present with you in spirit and delight to see how disciplined you are and how firm your faith in Christ is.

Colossians 2:4-5 New International Version

———⸻———

you can't r.u.n. if you don't

SHOW UP

To Those That Help Me R.U.N.

There were so many that said don't...but a *few* that said you must! For those few, here's to us operating in faith, walking in truth, braving the don'ts, and changing lives. Silence is the master assassinator of truth. Here's to truth, alive and well, with a bolstering voice.

To My God: thank you for the round trip ticket to hell and back (you know your child so I know you get it). Thank you for sustaining me when I couldn't find my way. It is my prayer that this journey empowers and emancipates others as I stand, unyielding, baring witness to Your power. Amen.

To Dollie: there's not a day that pasts that I don't miss you. Thank you for raising me to be the incredibly beautiful, strong, compassionate woman that I am. Thank you for your life, your love, your legacy. Everyday, I hope I make you proud.

To my children, all of you, thank you for your love, acceptance, and tolerance. You've traveled this rocky road with me and loved me nevertheless. Thank you for standing in faith with me as I share my truth. And thank you for not being ashamed of this truth. I am so blessed to have each of you.

To my husband: Ollie, you've been my rock, my life support, my friend, my after hours therapist, my snot rag, and a number of other things along this journey. Thank you for giving me hope in humanity again. And thank you for your undying love.

Julie, thank you for teaching me the beauty of being vulnerable and the strength behind being brave! You created for me a judgment free zone, for which I am eternally grateful. Because of you, I have the courage to not only own my story but the fortitude to share it with the entire world! Thank you for reminding me that I am "enough" and most importantly, thank you for saving and changing my life! May the God of ages always shine His grace upon you.

Bethany, I am humbly thankful for the strength, courage, and resilience you have spoken into my life. Just when I thought I'd conquered my traumas and figured everything out, life graced me with you as yet another reminder that God is incredible yet does have a remarkably interesting way of taking us to that next level. Thank you for your authentic self and for empowering me to be nothing less than fierce, confident, and resolute!

To my cousins, Shannon, Tabitha, and Tyneisha: since I was a little girl, you ladies have been my sisters. We have a bond that only God could create and I am so thankful He saw fit to weave the fabric of our lives together. You ladies have been a source of power when I have been weak and a true testament to what it means to stand in the balance. Thank you for loving me and always supporting me.

To Samantha and Diane, thank you for unselfishly sharing your journey. Thank you for your insight and information, freely given. May the road always rise to meet you.

Carolyn, thank you for giving me (and my sons) a roof over our heads when I had nowhere else to go. Thank you for love and friendship.

LaShon, thank you for the decades I've shared with you as a sister and friend. You've never judged me, never questioned my character, never asked me to redefine me. You truly accept all of me. To you, your mother, and your family, thank you.

To Alisa and Shawona: you physically reached into your pockets and gave me cash when I had almost nothing to call my own. You helped me pay my bills, make rent, and encouraged me to keep my head up when the enemy came in like a flood. Your friendship is everlasting and I am eternally thankful.

To Philena and James Williams: you showed up at the bank and deposited this unimaginable amount of money into my checking account when I was way past over drawn and had no idea how I would provide for my sons or myself in the face of such a turbulent and painful life altering ordeal. Even more so, you prayed for and with me every step of the way. Your kindness I have Never forgotten and I am eternally thankful.

To Ma Deannie and ReRe: you have been constant family to my sons and me. You have loved us, supported us, fed us, been our transportation...you've been whatever it is I have personally needed you to be. When I have been too weak to pray for myself, you've interceded. Your love is constant. Ma Deannie, I thank you for being a mother to me and ReRe, a sister. I thank The Most High God for you.

To my squad, my morning huddle chicks, Katerra, Summer, and Brittney: thank you for holding me down and lifting me up as only friendship can. Your continual support, prayers, love, motivation, and inspiration have not gone without notice and are a reflection of complete and infinite adoration. Katerra, you are the River. Thank you for constant intercession with the red phone. For each of your abounding friendships, I am ever grateful and love each of you dearly.

To Paris: I am ever grateful for our NEO connection and the pivotal role you've played in my life and that of my sons. Thank you for your love, acceptance, trust, and protection.

To Amanda Hyland: thank you for your counsel and for restoring true freedom unto me. You speak power to truth and I am forever thankful for your guidance. Because of you, this voice has a voice and gaslighting is, once again, exposed.

To Jan, Frank, and the entire Spoon family: I thank God for blessing our lives with each of you! Jan, you have loved us as your own and cared for our daughter accordingly. As I fumbled, you were there and as I waded through the waters, you cared for my sweet girl and me. I am eternally thankful.

My brother, life for us "ain't been no crystal stair".[86] But here we are, still "reachin' landin's".[87] You were my ride home from Greenleaf, a ride I'm ever thankful for. Thank you for supporting me through one of the most horrific times in my life. I love you always.

Olivia Grace: for every moment consumed, we shall uncover in this lifetime. God restores all as I'm confident that began through you. I love you sweet girl. May you always steer clear gaslighting.

Team Martin: thank you for your love and support. Candace, I praise God for your gifts and pray that He will always guide you and use you as the amazing vessel you are to spring forth the many talents embedded within you. Thank you for helping my vision find its voice.

To the Entire Prince Performance Publishing Family: thank you for giving me this opportunity to bring gaslighting center stage so that its noxious effects might be divested, lives might be saved, and the will of God be done. I am eternally thankful for Diane's leading me to you.

To the rest of the few that have accompanied me on this endless journey, let's not ever grow weary, not ever tire, not ever surrender ... let's R.U.N. Thank you.

Notes and References

PART I: CHAPTERS 1-6

1. Growe, R., & Montgomery, P. S. (2003). Educational Equity in America: Is Education the Great Equalizer? *The Professional Educator, XXV*(2), 23-29. Retrieved June 18, 2019 from https://files.eric.ed.gov/fulltext/EJ842412.pdf, p. 23.

PART II: CHAPTERS 7-17

2. About Dr. Thomas Gordon. (n.d.) Retrieved March 7, 2018 from http://www.gordontraining.com/thomas-gordon/about-dr-thomas-gordon-1918-2002/

3. The GoodTherapy.org Team. (2018 February 14). "I" Message [Web blog post]. Retrieved March 7, 2018 from https://www.goodtherapy.org/blog/psychpedia/i-message

4. Carson, C., & Holloran, P. (Eds.). (2000). A Knock at Midnight: Inspiration from the Great Sermons of Reverend Martin Luther King, Jr. New York: Warner Books, p. 32.

5. Chapman, Gary. (2015). The 5 Love Languages: The Secret to the Love that Lasts. Chicago, IL: Northfield Publishing.

6. Brown, B. (2012). Daring Greatly: How the Courage to be Vulnerable Transforms the Way We Live, Love, Parent, and Lead. New York: Gotham Books.

7. Steal [Def. 1]. In *Dictionary.com*. Retrieved April 4, 2018, from https:// dictionary.com/browse/steal.

8. Simon, G. (2010). In Sheep's Clothing, Revised Edition: Understanding and Dealing with Manipulative People. Marion, MI: Parkhurst Brothers, Inc., p. 153.

9. Kübler-Ross, E., & Kessler, D. (2014). On Grief & Grieving: Finding the Meaning of Grief Through the Five Stages of Loss. New York: Scribner.

PART III: CHAPTERS 18-22

10. Official Code of Georgia Annotated. (n.d.). Retrieved from https://law.justia.com/codes/georgia/2017/title-19/chapter-5/section-19-5-3/

11. Stern, R. (2018). The Gaslight Effect: How to Spot and Survive the Hidden Manipulation Others Use to Control Your Life. 1st ed., New York: Harmony Books, p. XXVI.

12. Process [Def. 1]. In Lexico.com. Retrieved August 31, 2019, from https://www.lexico.com/en/definition/process.

13. Simon, G. (2010). In Sheep's Clothing, Revised Edition: Understanding and Dealing with Manipulative People. Marion, MI: Parkhurst Brothers, Inc., p. 20.

14. Simon, G. (2010). In Sheep's Clothing, Revised Edition: Understanding and Dealing with Manipulative People. Marion, MI: Parkhurst Brothers, Inc., p. 16.

15. Simon, G. (2010). In Sheep's Clothing, Revised Edition: Understanding and Dealing with Manipulative People. Marion, MI: Parkhurst Brothers, Inc., pp. 16-17.

16. Simon, G. (2010). In Sheep's Clothing, Revised Edition: Understanding and Dealing with Manipulative People. Marion, MI: Parkhurst Brothers, Inc., p. 20.

17. Simon, G. (2010). In Sheep's Clothing, Revised Edition: Understanding and Dealing with Manipulative People. Marion, MI: Parkhurst Brothers, Inc., p. 63.

18. Simon, G. (2010). In Sheep's Clothing, Revised Edition: Understanding and Dealing with Manipulative People. Marion, MI: Parkhurst Brothers, Inc., p. 45.

19. Simon, G. (2010). In Sheep's Clothing, Revised Edition: Understanding and Dealing with Manipulative People. Marion, MI: Parkhurst Brothers, Inc., p. 44.

20. Simon, G. (2010). In Sheep's Clothing, Revised Edition: Understanding and Dealing with Manipulative People. Marion, MI: Parkhurst Brothers, Inc., p. 45.

21. Simon, G. (2010). In Sheep's Clothing, Revised Edition: Understanding and Dealing with Manipulative People. Marion, MI: Parkhurst Brothers, Inc., p. 130.

22. Simon, G. (2010). In Sheep's Clothing, Revised Edition: Understanding and Dealing with Manipulative People. Marion, MI: Parkhurst Brothers, Inc., p. 117.

23. Simon, G. (2010). In Sheep's Clothing, Revised Edition: Understanding and Dealing with Manipulative People. Marion, MI: Parkhurst Brothers, Inc., p. 126.

24. Simon, G. (2010). In Sheep's Clothing, Revised Edition: Understanding and Dealing with Manipulative People. Marion, MI: Parkhurst Brothers, Inc., p. 133.

25. Simon, G. (2010). In Sheep's Clothing, Revised Edition: Understanding and Dealing with Manipulative People. Marion, MI: Parkhurst Brothers, Inc., pp. 135-136.

26. Vulnerability. In *Oxford English Dictionary Online*. Retrieved May 7, 2019, from https://en.oxforddictionaries.com/definition/vulnerability.

27. Roosevelt, T. (1910). "Citizenship in a Republic," speech at the Sorbonne, Paris, April 23, 1910. Retrieved June 3, 2019 from http://www.theodore- roosevelt.com/images/research/speeches/maninthearena.pdf

28. Brown, B. (2012). Daring Greatly: How the Courage to be Vulnerable Transforms the Way We Live, Love, Parent, and Lead. New York: Gotham Books, p. 2.

29. Brown, B. (2012). Daring Greatly: How the Courage to be Vulnerable Transforms the Way We Live, Love, Parent, and Lead. New York: Gotham Books, p. 2.

30. Brown, B. (Presenter) & Fields, J. (Founder/Producer). (2014, November 25). Brené Brown: On Gratitude, Vulnerability and Courage [Audio Podcast]. Retrieved from Pandora

31. Brown, B. (2015). Rising Strong: The Reckoning. The Rumble. The Revolution. New York: Spiegel and Grau, p. 82.

32. Brown, B. (2012). Daring Greatly: How the Courage to be Vulnerable Transforms the Way We Live, Love, Parent, and Lead. New York: Gotham Books, p. 2.

33. Brown, B. (2012). Daring Greatly: How the Courage to be Vulnerable Transforms the Way We Live, Love, Parent, and Lead. New York: Gotham Books, p. 69.

34. Brown, B. (2015). Rising Strong: The Reckoning. The Rumble. The Revolution. New York: Spiegel and Grau, p. 225.

35. Brown, B. (2015). Rising Strong: The Reckoning. The Rumble. The Revolution. New York: Spiegel and Grau, p. 96.

36. Brown, B. (2012). Daring Greatly: How the Courage to be Vulnerable Transforms the Way We Live, Love, Parent, and Lead. New York: Gotham Books, p. 67.

37. Brown, B. (2015). Rising Strong: The Reckoning. The Rumble. The Revolution. New York: Spiegel and Grau, p. xx.

38. Brown, B. (2015). Rising Strong: The Reckoning. The Rumble. The Revolution. New York: Spiegel and Grau, p. 75.

PART IV: CHAPTERS 23-24

39. Black, T., Fox, J., & Washington, D. (Producers), Gilroy, D. (Director). 2017. *Roman J. Israel, Esq* [Motion Picture]. United States: Cross Creek Pictures.

40. "Beautiful Trauma." Moore, A., Antonoff, J. (2017). RCA Records.

41. Brown, B. (2015). Rising Strong: The Reckoning. The Rumble. The Revolution. New York: Spiegel and Grau, p. 241.

42. Brown, B. (2015). Rising Strong: The Reckoning. The Rumble. The Revolution. New York: Spiegel and Grau, p. 249.

43. Brown, B. (2015). Rising Strong: The Reckoning. The Rumble. The Revolution. New York: Spiegel and Grau, p. 6.

44. Pinsky, R., & Dietz, M. (Eds.). (2000). Americans' Favorite Poems: The Favorite Poem Project Anthology. New York: W. W. Norton & Company, Inc., pp. 114-115.

45. Pinsky, R., & Dietz, M. (Eds.). (2000). Americans' Favorite Poems: The Favorite Poem Project Anthology. New York: W. W. Norton & Company, Inc., pp. 114-115.

46. Feige, K. (Producer), Coogler, R. (Director). 2018. *Black Panther* [Motion picture]. United States: Marvel Studios.

47. Feige, K. (Producer), Coogler, R. (Director). 2018. *Black Panther* [Motion picture]. United States: Marvel Studios.

48. Feige, K. (Producer), Coogler, R. (Director). 2018. *Black Panther* [Motion picture]. United States: Marvel Studios.

49. Feige, K. (Producer), Coogler, R. (Director). 2018. *Black Panther* [Motion picture]. United States: Marvel Studios.

50. Black, T., Blumenthal, J., Washington, D., Siskin, A., Tisch, S., Fuqua, A., Neufeld, M., Eldridge, T., Sloan, M. (Producers), Fuqua, A. (Director). 2018. *The Equalizer 2* [Motion picture]. United States: Columbia Pictures.

51. Brown, B. (2015). Rising Strong: The Reckoning. The Rumble. The Revolution. New York: Spiegel and Grau, p. 4.

52. Simon, G. (2010). In Sheep's Clothing, Revised Edition: Understanding and Dealing with Manipulative People. Marion, MI: Parkhurst Brothers, Inc., p. 143.

53. Simon, G. (2010). In Sheep's Clothing, Revised Edition: Understanding and Dealing with Manipulative People. Marion, MI: Parkhurst Brothers, Inc., p. 138.

54. Simon, G. (2010). In Sheep's Clothing, Revised Edition: Understanding and Dealing with Manipulative People. Marion, MI: Parkhurst Brothers, Inc., p. 143.

55. Simon, G. (2010). In Sheep's Clothing, Revised Edition: Understanding and Dealing with Manipulative People. Marion, MI: Parkhurst Brothers, Inc., p. 144.

56. Simon, G. (2010). In Sheep's Clothing, Revised Edition: Understanding and Dealing with Manipulative People. Marion, MI: Parkhurst Brothers, Inc., p. 144.

57. Simon, G. (2010). In Sheep's Clothing, Revised Edition: Understanding and Dealing with Manipulative People. Marion, MI: Parkhurst Brothers, Inc., p. 145.

58. Brown, B. (2015). Rising Strong: The Reckoning. The Rumble. The Revolution. New York: Spiegel and Grau, p. 244.

59. Brown, B. (2015). Rising Strong: The Reckoning. The Rumble. The Revolution. New York: Spiegel and Grau, p. 244.

60. "King of Anything": Bareilles, S. (2010) "King of Anything," on Kaleidoscope Heart, Epic Records.

61. Simon, G. (2010). In Sheep's Clothing, Revised Edition: Understanding and Dealing with Manipulative People. Marion, MI: Parkhurst Brothers, Inc., p. 147.

62. Simon, G. (2010). In Sheep's Clothing, Revised Edition: Understanding and Dealing with Manipulative People. Marion, MI: Parkhurst Brothers, Inc., p. 157.

63. Simon, G. (2010). In Sheep's Clothing, Revised Edition: Understanding and Dealing with Manipulative People. Marion, MI: Parkhurst Brothers, Inc., pp. 137-137.

64. Simon, G. (2010). In Sheep's Clothing, Revised Edition: Understanding and Dealing with Manipulative People. Marion, MI: Parkhurst Brothers, Inc., p. 137.

FINAL THOUGHTS

65. Brown, B. (2015). Rising Strong: The Reckoning. The Rumble. The Revolution. New York: Spiegel and Grau, p. 83.

66. Brown, B. (2015). Rising Strong: The Reckoning. The Rumble. The Revolution. New York: Spiegel and Grau, p. 202.

67. Holmes, T. (2011). Parts Work: An Illustrated Guide to Your Inner Life. 4th Ed., Michigan: Winged Heart Press, p. 1.

68. Holmes, T. (2011). Parts Work: An Illustrated Guide to Your Inner Life. 4th Ed., Michigan: Winged Heart Press, p. 2.

69. Schwartz, R. (1987). Our Multiple Selves: Applying Systems Thinking to the Inner Family. *Family Therapy Networker*, 21-31. Retrieved June 20, 2019 from https://hakomiinstitute.com/Forum/Issue10/OurMultipleSelves.pdf, p. 23.

70. Holmes, T. (2011). Parts Work: An Illustrated Guide to Your Inner Life. 4th Ed., Michigan: Winged Heart Press, p. 31.

71. Holmes, T. (2011). Parts Work: An Illustrated Guide to Your Inner Life. 4th Ed., Michigan: Winged Heart Press, p.41.

72. Holmes, T. (2011). Parts Work: An Illustrated Guide to Your Inner Life. 4th Ed., Michigan: Winged Heart Press, p. 2.

73. Holmes, T. (2011). Parts Work: An Illustrated Guide to Your Inner Life. 4th Ed., Michigan: Winged Heart Press, p. 18.

74. Holmes, T. (2011). Parts Work: An Illustrated Guide to Your Inner Life. 4th Ed., Michigan: Winged Heart Press, p. 17.

75. Holmes, T. (2011). Parts Work: An Illustrated Guide to Your Inner Life. 4th Ed., Michigan: Winged Heart Press, p. 17.

76. Holmes, T. (2011). Parts Work: An Illustrated Guide to Your Inner Life. 4th Ed., Michigan: Winged Heart Press, p. 5.

77. Holmes, T. (2011). Parts Work: An Illustrated Guide to Your Inner Life. 4th Ed., Michigan: Winged Heart Press, p. 6.

78. Holmes, T. (2011). Parts Work: An Illustrated Guide to Your Inner Life. 4th Ed., Michigan: Winged Heart Press, p. 6.

79. Holmes, T. (2011). Parts Work: An Illustrated Guide to Your Inner Life. 4th Ed., Michigan: Winged Heart Press, p. 10.

80. Schwartz, R. (n.d.). Evolution of the Internal Family Systems Model. Retrieved June 21, 2019 from https://www.selfleadership.org/about-internal-family-systems.html

81. Schwartz, R. (n.d.). Evolution of the Internal Family Systems Model. Retrieved June 21, 2019 from https://www.selfleadership.org/about-internal-family-systems.html, para. 7.

82. Schwartz, R. (n.d.). Evolution of the Internal Family Systems Model. Retrieved June 21, 2019 from https://www.selfleadership.org/about-internal-family-systems.html, para. 8.

83. Schwartz, R. (n.d.). Evolution of the Internal Family Systems Model. Retrieved June 21, 2019 from https://www.selfleadership.org/about-internal-family-systems.html, para. 8.

84. Holmes, T. (2011). Parts Work: An Illustrated Guide to Your Inner Life. 4th Ed., Michigan: Winged Heart Press, pp. 99-101.

85. Brown, B. (2015). Rising Strong: The Reckoning. The Rumble. The Revolution. New York: Spiegel and Grau, p. 267.

TO THOSE THAT HELP ME R.U.N.

86. Hughes, L. (1990). Selected Poems of Langston Hughes: A Classic Collection of Poems by a Master of American Verse. New York: Vintage Classics, p. 187.

87. Hughes, L. (1990). Selected Poems of Langston Hughes: A Classic Collection of Poems by a Master of American Verse. New York: Vintage Classics, p. 187.

Kemberley is a native of Augusta, Georgia, and is a proud graduate of Augusta's Historically Black College and University (HBCU), Paine College. During her years at Paine, she pledged Delta Sigma Theta Sorority, Incorporated, and served the college as Miss Paine College 2000-2001. After graduating as salutatorian, Kemberley went on to achieve her Doctor of Pharmacy degree from The University of Georgia College of Pharmacy. Subsequently, she completed a postgraduate residency program at Northeast Georgia Health System and has since served the practice of pharmacy in a myriad of capacities, including Clinical Assistant Professor for the department of Psychiatry and Behavioral Health for the Medical College of Georgia (Augusta University). Some of her most valued experiences are those shared with her patients as pain medicine specialist and specialist in opioid-substance use disorder treatment. Today, Kemberley resides in Evans, Georgia, with her husband, Ollie. Together, they are the blessed parents of seven amazing children.

www.ingramcontent.com/pod-product-compliance
Lightning Source LLC
Chambersburg PA
CBHW020251130626

46549CB00005B/2163